THE OVERLAND LAUNCH

THE OVERLAND LAUNCH

Written and illustrated by

C. Walter Hodges

EXMOOR BOOKS
Published in association with Exmoor National Park Authority

First published by G. Bell & Sons Ltd 1969
First published in the New Windmill Series 1975
This edition published by Exmoor Books 1990

ISBN: 0 86183–181–0

British Library Cataloguing-in-Publication Data
CIP Catalogue Record for this book is available from the British Library.

Printed and bound in Great Britain
by BPCC Wheatons Ltd, Exeter

EXMOOR BOOKS
Official Publisher to Exmoor National Park Authority
An imprint of Wheaton Publishers Ltd
A member of the Maxwell Communication Corporation plc

Wheaton Publishers Ltd
Hennock Road, Exeter, Devon EX2 8RP
Tel: 0392 411131

SALES
Direct sales enquiries to Exmoor Books at the address above

PREFACE

THIS is a true story. That is to say, all the main events described in it did in fact occur, as here related, at the time and for the reasons given. A brief account of the incident, as told by Coxswain G. S. Richards when he was an old man, was published in the Life-Boat Journal for September 1933. Coxswain Richards was Second Coxswain in the Lynmouth life-boat at the time of the incident. His younger brother William, who was a well-known character in Lynmouth until only a few years ago, accompanied him in the boat, it being his first service. I have talked to people who remember both of them, and other members of the crew, very well. I have also made it my business to walk all the way the life-boat went on the night of the incident. The road has been very much widened since then, and is now well made up (which in the old days it could not be, for the hills were too steep for the old steam-rollers) but otherwise nothing much has changed. Only it was a fine spring day, not a black stormy January night, when I walked that way.

But though this is a true story, it cannot be said that nothing has been added, nothing taken away. It is now nearly seventy years since the event. Even the hardest facts are dissolved with time, and if facts alone were to be taken into account what remains about this incident could all, I suppose, be fairly easily written down on two or three sheets of paper. Anything beyond that must be either comment or imagination; and since in my handwriting this account covers some hundred pages, it will be seen that I must have added, for better or worse, quite an amount of imagination. As for the taking away, this, as I have just said, was not done by me, but by time. The event being over, nothing can replace, for those who merely hear about it in comfort afterwards, the true sense of what it was like to be there at the time, when the outcome of it all was still unknown. Nothing can really make us feel what it is like to do hard physical work for twenty hours at a stretch in a storm of bitter cold, being all the time wet through to the skin, and with some possibility that you might be drowned in the end. Only by the use of imagination can one put back something which may partly take the place of such vivid and immediate feelings. I offer this as at least a partial excuse for the additions and alterations I have made.

It may be useful if I state briefly what these are. To begin with, it will at once be understood that if one is writing an account, supposed to be true, of some historical incident, and if in the middle of it one makes up speeches to fit the event, and puts them into the mouths of characters who were once real people taking part in the real event, nothing is more certain than that they did *not* say just those words, just there or just then. The speeches are imaginary, only carefully designed to give an *effect* of truth and reality. And so at that point the so-called 'history' has begun to cease being true, and is beginning to become a work of fiction with a life of its own. I have done this here. And since, because of this among other things, my account was already starting to become a work of half-fiction, I have gone two steps further. First, I have added one or two wholly fictional characters, purely for the sake of my story-telling; and second, I have deliberately altered (but usually only rather slightly) the names of the real people of the story. I have done this for the sake of consistency, and to give myself the full liberty of the fictional technique I have chosen to use (as, for instance, in the use of conversations). But it would be very wrong if the true names of the life-boatmen of Lynmouth who conducted this brave enterprise should not appear in this book. I therefore print their names below, and would like respectfully to dedicate the story to their memory. I also hope their surviving relatives, should any of them read this, will excuse any errors and inventions of characterization they may find.

Lastly, I would here like to thank the Royal National Life-boat Institution, and also Mr. Tom F. Bevan, who was the Institution's last Honorary Secretary at Lynmouth before that life-boat station was closed in 1944, for all the help and advice they have given me.

Here are the names of the Lynmouth life-boat crew on the night of the 12th January 1899: John Crocombe (Coxswain), George Richards (Second-coxswain), Richard Ridler (Bowman), Richard Burgess, Charles Crick, David Crocombe, William Jarvis, Bertram Pennicott, Thomas Pugsley, George Rawle, William Richards, John Ridler, John Ward and Richard Moore (Signalman). Mr. E. J. Pedder, the Lynmouth post master at that time, also sailed in the boat.

Bishopstone, 1968.

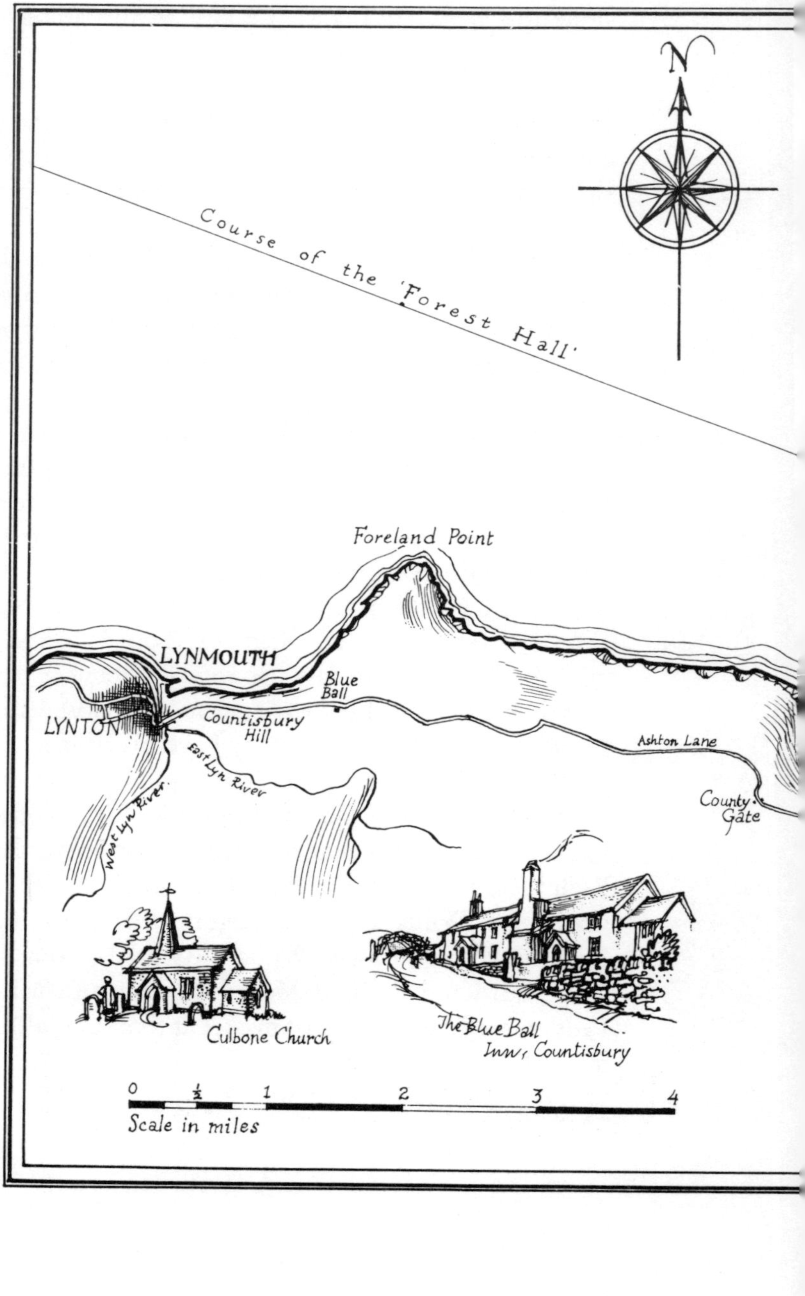
N
Course of the 'Forest Hall'
Foreland Point
LYNMOUTH
Blue Ball
LYNTON
Countisbury Hill
East Lyn River
West Lyn River
Ashton Lane
County Gate
Culbone Church
The Blue Ball Inn, Countisbury
0 ½ 1 2 3 4
Scale in miles

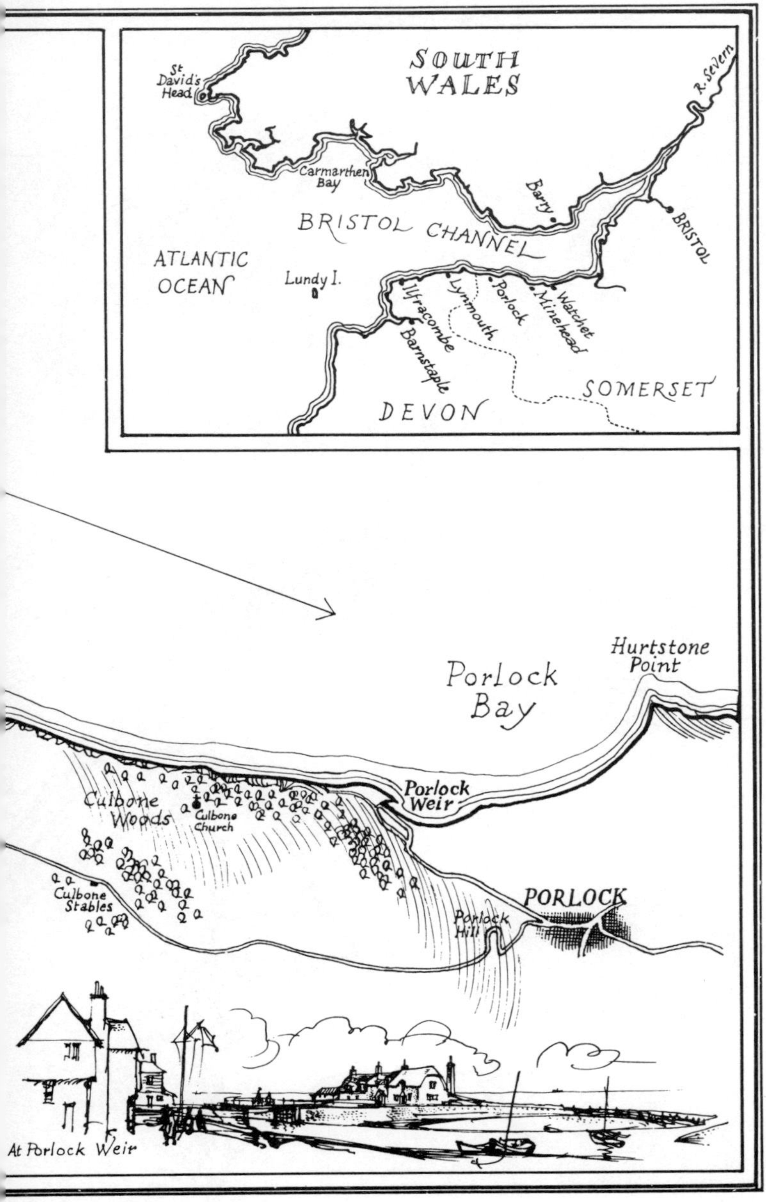

SOUTH WALES
St David's Head
Carmarthen Bay
Barry
R. Severn
BRISTOL
BRISTOL CHANNEL
ATLANTIC OCEAN
Lundy I.
Ilfracombe
Barnstaple
Lynmouth
Porlock
Minehead
Watchet
DEVON
SOMERSET
Hurtstone Point
Porlock Bay
Porlock Weir
Culbone Woods
Culbone Church
Culbone Stables
Porlock Hill
PORLOCK
At Porlock Weir

STEEP HILL
STOP!
ENGAGE BOTTOM
GEAR NOW

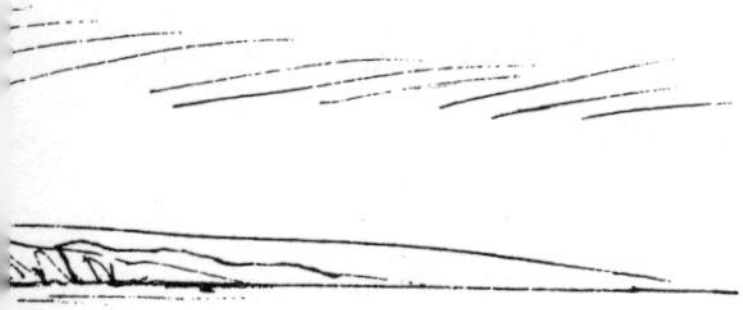

CHAPTER ONE

ONE in four-and-a-half is a very steep hill. Going down from Exmoor to Lynmouth by Countisbury Hill the road descends a thousand feet in less than two miles. The gradients go from one in seven to one in five, and at last to one in four-and-a-half. All the way down, the moorland drops steeply away on the right, over to the cliff edge and the sea. Far below, the gulls float and circle over the waves, and the moorland sheep, grazing along the edge of the precipice, look down on them from above.

Motorists beginning the descent are given plenty of warning. 'STEEP HILL', says a large notice-board at the top: 'STOP! ENGAGE BOTTOM GEAR NOW.' The notice is repeated a little further down for the benefit of sceptics and slow readers. At the same time cyclists are advised to dismount and walk. Further down still, other notices are repeated: 'Escape Road for Vehicles Out of Control: 200 yards on left.' The escape roads are short tracks cut into the hillside and filled with sand, into which you can run for safety when your brakes give out. It is forbidden to park in them and they are nearly always empty. Cars travelling in low gear arrive safely at the bottom of the long hill, and then, with a half turn over the bridge, there they are in Lynmouth.

It is still one of the prettiest places in England. Even to-day you can still see this little Devonshire fishing village very much as it used to be two hundred years ago, when the painter Gainsborough praised it for its romantic scenery; or when, a little later, the poet Shelley went to stay there. The little old thatched cottages are still there; the short, narrow street of little shops, which is simply called Lynmouth Street, is still hemmed in between the harbour on one side and the cliff-steep hill on the other. It has no room to change. The harbour still has its fishing boats and lobster-pots; and the two rivers, the East and the West Lyn, which some think are the prettiest rivers in the West Country, still come in and meet there just below the bridge, and run out together through the harbour mouth. These rivers come down from Exmoor through steep-sided, tree-shaded glens, bubbling over rocks, sliding smoothly over pools where fishes lurk and rest, all the way between banks green with moss and ferns. The paths along the riverside still lead to pretty farms and villages not far inland. But of course, in the holiday season nowadays these leafy walks are not so solitary as once they were. There are so many people, and the car-parks in Lynmouth are always full. But then it is such a pretty place who would not wish to come and see it?

Perhaps the best time of all to have seen it would have been about the end of the last century, or the beginning of this one—just the time, in fact, when the events of this story took place. Since travelling was not so easy then as it is now, there were fewer visitors, but there were many enough, and those who came stayed longer. Well-to-do Victorian gentlemen built their well-to-do Victorian

houses on the high hill right above the village, in the sister-village of Lynton, which looks across the valley to Countisbury. Lynmouth is ringed in with high hills, and because of this it reminded the Victorian gentry who settled there of romantic places they had seen in their travels abroad, of scenes by mountain lakes in Switzerland, or on the River Rhine. To assist the Rhineland effect a generous resident had given the money to build on the jetty a little watch-tower, copying the style of castle towers in mediaeval Germany. It served (and still serves) as a lighthouse.

Other improvements were made. A cliff railway was built, to link Lynton above with Lynmouth below, thus at last doing away with the long, tiring zig-zag walk up the hill, or the donkey-ride which was the only alternative to this in earlier times. The cliff railway was considered a wonder. It had two cars balanced against each other on a long cable, each carrying a water-tank which, being filled and emptied alternately, took the cars up and down the rails by gravity. This, too, is still at work, and we may ride in it, and step out at the top as our grandparents and great-grandparents did, and admire the fine view from up there, of Lynmouth Bay, of wild Exmoor over Countisbury Hill, of the Bristol Channel and, beyond it, on a clear day, the distant coast of Wales. In those earlier days (but not now, alas) at holiday time you would also have seen the long-funnelled, gay-painted, brass-fitted paddle-steamer coming round from Minehead into Lynmouth Bay, churning up a broad white road of foam behind her big paddle-boxes and sounding a long blast on her siren as she came near. She came to take the holiday people for trips along the coast to Ilfracombe and Clovelly. But the approaches to Lynmouth are shallow and rocky, and so she never came close in. As soon as she was seen rounding the Foreland into the Bay, the Lynmouth boatmen used to push off from the quayside with the passengers and pull away to a point two hundred yards beyond low-water mark, where the steamer would meet them. They used very large rowing boats, specially built for the purpose, twenty-five and thirty feet long, and they were pulled with two or three pairs of oars. It was all quite a to-do. The boats were very spick and span because of the passengers' holiday clothes, the ladies all in their best white blouses, with their ankle-length skirts and their wide flowery hats and their frilled sunshades, which were pretty enough to look at but not very easy to manage while still keeping one hand free for the boatman to hand them aboard when they got out to the ship, all rocking on the open sea.

And the boatmen! In those days they seemed to be men of a different world altogether, hardly the same species of mankind as the summer passengers they rowed in their boats. They wore thick patched trousers, thick dark jerseys and thick woollen caps. They had thick rough beards. They smoked thick strong tobacco in little broken-off clay pipes, and they spoke with warm, rough Devonshire accents. Their faces were weathered and sun-tanned and dark, quite unlike the faces of the holiday people who, in those days, did not like to 'catch the sun', and walked in the shade when ever they could. Of an evening the holiday people used to like to stroll along the harbour wall, and watch these strange fishermen at their picturesque work, mending nets or tarring boats, or even bringing in a catch. The visitors considered them all to be what they called 'old salts', and liked to think they all had unbelievable stories to tell about their life at sea; and it was believed these stories could be coaxed out of them with a pint of ale in the tap-room of the 'Rising Sun'. Perhaps they could. One or two of the Lynmouth boatmen had in fact been deep-sea sailors at one time or another. There was Jack Lord, for one, who had sailed round the Horn in a windjammer when he was younger. It would not have been beyond him to talk about it to interested visitors, by way of being sociable. But for the most part they were longshore fishermen. Some, like Tom Tugsley, Jack Crockham, and Dick Vidler, had their own boats and carried cargoes between the Devon and Somerset ports and over to Wales. Not a great distance, it may be thought. But they were all experienced seamen. The Bristol Channel is not the easiest water to sail, and in bad

weather it can be very bad indeed. The local people knew all about that. It was not for nothing there was a life-boat stationed at Lynmouth.

The summer visitors, when they had done strolling along the harbour-side and talking to the fishermen, would often pause on their way back to their hotels, and take an interested peep through the windows of the life-boat house. Or with any luck there might be a crewman on duty, and the doors might be open. Or with better luck still the boat might be standing out on the quay, ready for a wash-down and inspection.

Always clean and bright, ready and waiting, the Lynmouth life-boat stood mounted on her launching carriage. She was a pulling and sailing life-boat, 34 feet 3 inches in

length, and 7 feet 6 inches in breadth. She weighed $3\frac{1}{2}$ tons, unladen. She was pulled with ten oars and rigged with two masts and lugsails, though her masts were not usually stepped till she was ready for launching. She was self-righting—that is, if she were to capsize she would roll over and up again. She had recently been refitted and improved, with new water-ballast tanks, new end-boxes, a new iron keel, and new pumps. Thus (for this was before the days of motor-driven life-boats) she could consider herself the equal of any boat in the service. Her name was *Louisa*.

When mounted on her launching-carriage her keel was carried on a keelway 22 feet long, which was fitted with eleven steel rollers. On these rollers the whole weight of the boat rested. The keelway itself was carried on the main axle-bed, and this in turn was supported by two great wheels, seven feet high, and overall nearly ten feet apart, which flanked the boat amidships. Amidships also, one on each side of the keelway, were two long strakes, called bilge-pieces, which made a sort of cradle for her to rest in.

The forward part of the carriage consisted of two four-foot wheels mounted on a fore-carriage and turntable, which was attached so that it pivoted under the fore-end of the keelway. Two pairs of shafts were provided, for fitting to this fore-carriage, so that the whole carriage and life-boat could be drawn by horses to the launching place, should this ever be needed. But at Lynmouth there had never been such a need, nor was one ever to be foreseen. The distance to the launching beach was only two hundred yards. The carriage was therefore always man-handled, hauled by drag-ropes attached to the fore-carriage, and to rings in the axle-naves of the great launching wheels. There was never any lack of hands for hauling. The horse-shafts were kept in the boat house unused.

To place the boat on the carriage, the whole fore-carriage was detached and taken away, and the keelway allowed to slope downwards with its forward end resting on the ground. The boat was then pushed up on the keelway rollers, and firmly secured by chains which passed through holes in the boat's keel, fore and aft. The keelway was then jacked up, and the fore-carriage brought back into position under it. The boat travelled on the carriage stern foremost. This was because of the normal method of launching, as will be seen.

Sometimes the summer visitors would have the good

fortune to see the life-boat being launched for an exercise. It made a very pleasant spectacle, a nice diversion for a fine evening. It would start when Dick Morley, the life-boat Signalman, fired three signal rockets, at minute intervals, from a firing point on the harbour wall. They exploded with three loud bangs over the harbour, and echoed away in the high hills all round. At once, from every part of the village some eighteen to twenty enrolled life-boatmen would drop whatever else they were doing, hurry into their sea-clothes, and run full pelt for the boat-house, where a row of life-jackets hanging on the wall awaited the first comers. A full crew for the boat was thirteen. The first three, the Coxswain, Second Coxswain and Bowman, were permanent officers. For the remainder the rule was that the first ten to reach the boat-house got the jackets. Usually in daylight it took between five and ten minutes to muster a crew; at night, a little longer.

But when the rocket went up it was the whole population of the village, or so it seemed, that hurried to life-boat house. There were not only the crew but the launchers, who would include any capable person, man or woman, boatman or shopkeeper, who was willing and able to lay a hand on the drag-ropes. In summertime even the gentlemen visitors liked to help, perhaps remembering that Sir Francis Drake had made it his rule that 'the gentlemen should haul with the mariners'. And by the time the boat was out on the quay, which was not long, there would be a large and ever-increasing crowd of spectators to follow her along to the launching-place. Riding in the boat to make all ready and step the masts as she went along would be Second Coxswain George Pritchard, and Dick Vidler the Bowman.

At the top of the slope which ran down to the beach,

the carriage was turned about, so that the bow and the big launching wheels were towards the sea, and in this position it was run down onto the beach. Here Coxswain Jack Crockham and the rest of the crew climbed aboard. All bulky in the great cork life-jackets they wore in those days, seated in their places with their oars held upright, they looked strangely heroic, like a boatload of tough old armoured knights with their lances, being carted off to a tournament. Thus the launchers ran them down into the water as deep as they could go.

Here what happened was this. The keelway with its rollers, now in its reversed position, had a downward slope towards the sea: it was, in fact, a launching slip. The two chains which secured the boat's keel to the slipway were released. The bow chain was pulled clear, but the stern chain had a long rope attached to the end of it, and this rope, called the 'strop', was held securely by the Second Coxswain. Thus the whole launch was now literally in his hands. The launchers on each side stood down in the water holding the launching ropes, ready to give the haul which would send the boat off down the slip. George Pritchard with the strop in his hand waited for the moment when a good lifting wave came in and flooded round the boat. Then he shouted 'Haul!' and let go the strop, and the launchers hauled. The strop ran out through the keel hole as the life-boat *Louisa* shot down the slipway and out with the wave into deeper water, her oars striking the sea all together, her bow rising into the next oncoming wave with a great dash of foam. Once out beyond this, she was well launched and away. The summer visitors cheered and waved their handerchiefs, and no wonder, for it was a gallant sight to see.

But it was very much more gallant sometimes when fewer visitors, if any, would be there to watch. To launch in rough weather against heavy seas was a hard, skilful and hazardous operation. Unless it were well managed the boat could be swept back and turned over. It always was well managed, but not always easily.

Among the Lynmouth boys who came to watch and lend a hand where they could, winter or summer, were young Billy Pritchard, brother of Second Coxswain George, and his friend Derry Larkins.

Derry was thirteen. He had left school a year ago, and was now working as a stable-boy at Mr. Tom Jonas's coaching stables up in Lynton. He liked it very much.

But Lynmouth people, whatever other jobs they may have, are always half seafaring people at heart, and so was he. His father had been a fisherman; but he had been drowned when his boat capsized in a storm, when Derry was only seven. Since then Derry's mother had worked in the hotels and let lodgings in her house to make ends meet, and when Derry left school and went out to work it had been a great help to her. But she wouldn't let him work in the boats. He was the only one of his friends who did not.

Billy Pritchard, who lived in the cottage next door to Derry's, was an older boy. He was sixteen. He was by this time already a seasoned and experienced sailor. He sailed in Dick Vidler's ketch, mostly working along the coast between Ilfracombe and Watchet. Since Dick Vidler was, as we have seen, Bowman in the life-boat, and since Billy's brother George was Second Cox, it was hardly surprising that Billy had already put his name down for enrolment in the life-boat crew.

The Reverend Oakley, Vicar of St. John's Church, who was the Life-boat Institution's Honorary Secretary at Lynmouth, was inclined to think that sixteen was rather too young, and that Billy ought to wait a year. But life-boatmen tend to go in families. There was Coxswain Jack Crockham and his brother Dave; there was Dick Vidler and his brother Jack; so why not George Pritchard's brother Billy? Billy was as good as enrolled already.

Secretly Derry Larkins found himself hoping his friend might have to wait a little longer. There was in any case a large gap in age between them. Billy had already started calling Derry 'young 'un'. Once in the life-boat he would finally have crossed over the invisible line and joined the men. Derry would still be only a boy, and it would be years before he could catch up with his friend again.

Nevertheless, one fine evening in late autumn, when the life-boat was being washed down and her equipment inspected on the quay outside the boat-house, George Pritchard, who was in charge, saw his brother and called out to him:

'There you are, then, Billy, what'd I tell you? Mr. Oakley's just been here and he says you're enrolled. You'd better come over here right away and try on for a jacket. Always ready for service from now on, Billy me lad! It might be any time.'

As it happened, Billy's first service, when it came, was to be the strangest in his long lifetime.

CHAPTER TWO

BY THE middle of October the last of the summer visitors were packing their trunks and taking their places on the stage-coach for Minehead, eighteen miles away, there to catch the train. In those days there was, as an alternative, a narrow-gauge single-track railway which ran from Lynton to meet the main line at Barnstaple, but that was a long way round; and besides in fine weather it made a pleasanter farewell to the holiday to take the coach. They were four-horse coaches, with two additional horses used for the steep ascent of Countisbury Hill; but even with this help, if there was a heavy load it was sometimes necessary for the gentlemen passengers to get out and walk at the steepest places. Then, the hill being surmounted, there would be the gay trot-along over Exmoor, with a last view of the Doone Valley below, and the grand panorama of the sea and the steep granite coastline at County Gate where the road passes from Devon into Somerset; and then the sharp descent of Porlock Hill, steeper even than Countisbury and complicated with dangerous bends; and so after that to Minehead, and goodbye. All comes to an end, and back in Lynmouth the people are on their own again, getting ready for the winter.

The coaches and horses on the Minehead run all belonged to Mr. Jonas of Lynton. He had a large stable, and his people were kept on the go all day. During the season Derry Larkins worked from eight in the morning till eight at night, fetching fodder and litter, saddling up, brushing down, mucking out, and polishing harness between whiles. And when he wasn't needed at Lynton he would be sent to Mr. Jonas's staging stables at Culbone, over towards Porlock, where the Minehead coach changed horses.

Derry always liked going to Culbone. It was a pretty place in a tree-sheltered hollow on the moor, and many people from Lynmouth and Porlock used to go there to walk in the woods and visit the tiny parish church, which is only 35 feet long, a mere eight inches longer than the life-boat at Lynmouth, and is the smallest complete parish church in England. Besides which, there used to be at one time, near the church, a place called Brimstone Farm, where the poet Coleridge was staying when he wrote his poem *Kubla Khan*. The story is well-known, how he dreamed the whole poem complete in his sleep, and, on waking, started quickly to write it down while it was all still vivid in his mind. But then, as he explained afterwards, in the middle of it he was interrupted by somebody he called 'a person from Porlock'; and when this innocently blundering person had gone, so had the rest of the poem. Derry had heard this story many times. Literary visitors used to tell it to him or to each other when they were asking him the way to the no longer existing Brimstone Farm. He had also been told about it at school, as he remembered.

'It's funny, though, ain't it?' he said. 'I mean, people coming all this way to see a place that ain't there any more, where somebody didn't finish a poem more than a hundred years ago.'

He said this to Mr. Stringston as they were riding back on the last coach from Culbone one afternoon in early November. He had been sent to Culbone to help the ostler check the harness that had been left there, now that nearly all the horses had been taken back to Lynton, and to bring back with him anything that needed repairing over the winter. He had it all in a sack in the coach. It was a showery, blustery day, the road was all muddy and full of dead leaves, and he and the sack and Mr. Stringston were the only occupants of the coach.

Mr. Stringston was a good-natured man of nearly thirty who was an assistant teacher up at Lynton School, where Derry used to go until his twelfth birthday, when, naturally, he had left. Twelve was the leaving age in those days. Mr. Stringston didn't think it was enough. During term-time he lodged in Derry's mother's house, and often used to talk to her about the education of children and how he thought it ought to be done. If he had his way, he said, boys like Derry would be kept at school till they were at least fourteen, whether they liked it or not.

'Would *you* have liked it?' he asked Derry. Derry replied politely that he wouldn't have minded.

Mr. Stringston was coming back from some business he had to do in Porlock on this particular afternoon, when Derry and his bundle got into the coach at Culbone. As they went along Derry was telling him about his summer's work, and about all the visitors; and it was then he came out with his thought about Coleridge at Brimstone Farm.

'Funny, ain't it?' he repeated. 'After all, just one poem, and not finished neither.'

'Why are you surprised?' Mr. Stringston asked. 'There are many people who like poetry very much, and *Kubla Khan* is a favourite with nearly everyone. I thought you used to like that sort of thing yourself once, when you were at school.'

'Well, yes,' said Derry. 'It's nice. I like it. But I like they properly written stories better. I like some of they Old Testament stories very much, which Mr. Oakley reads in the First Lesson, in church. Were you there last Sunday, Mr. Stringston? We 'ad it from the Book of Judges, all about Barak and Sisera and all 'is chariots of iron. 'E 'ad nine 'undred of 'em, Mr. Stringston, nine 'undred. And when 'e lost the battle 'e got down and run off, and 'e went and 'id 'isself in the tent of a woman called Jael, the wife of 'Eber the Kenite. Do you know that story?'

'Yes', said Mr. Stringston; 'he asked her for water and she gave him milk to drink.'

'Yes', said Derry, 'and then she went and got a tent-peg and struck it through 'is 'ead.'

The coach joggled on for a while, and neither of them spoke. Then Derry said:

'I used to like all them stories you told us in school, too, Mr. Stringston. Them about Ooly-Sees.'

'Ooly . . . ?' Mr. Stringston began, and then 'Ah, yes. Ulysses. You liked them, you say?'

'Yes, I did, very much. And Pozzidon and Yolus, them gods. I liked them a lot. I liked it that time when Yolus gave Ooly-Sees all them winds tied up in a bag, to 'elp 'im along. And then Ooly's men let 'em all out by mistake, and there was that big storm.'

'Poseidon and Aeolus, the gods of the waves and the winds. Yes,' Mr. Stringston said, 'I remember. But fancy *you* remembering.'

'Oh, I do,' said Derry. 'Funny 'ow it sticks in yer 'ead, ain't it? But what I can't never remember is, why was it ol' Pozzidon was so set against Ooly-Sees? 'E wouldn't let 'im 'ave no luck at all, would 'e? Chased after 'im and wouldn't let 'im go 'ome for ten years. What'd Ooly done?'

'He'd done harm to Poseidon's son,' Mr. Stringston answered. 'Do you remember the giant Polyphemus, the one with the single eye in the middle of his forehead?'

'Oh, 'im, yes,' said Derry. 'Ooly and 'is men poked it out with a stick, didn't they? Well, it was really like a gurt big pole, wasn't it, and they'd 'ardened a point on it in the fire. Mind you, that ol' giant was goin' to eat 'em all alive; so they 'ad to do *some*thing.'

'Quite so,' said Mr. Stringston; 'but as it happened, that old giant was the sea-god Poseidon's favourite son, and when he was blinded by Ulysses he called on his father to revenge him. So Poseidon, too, had to do something; and so he pursued Ulysses ever afterwards, wherever he went, doing him all the harm he could.'

Derry said: 'Ah, well, then, that explains it, don't it? I've 'eard there *are* people like that, too; bad luck follows 'em wherever they go, as if them ol' gods was after 'em.' He paused a moment, then he went on, 'I'll tell you something, Mr. Stringston. You know what I sometimes think?'

Mr. Stringston didn't. Derry leaned forward in the seat opposite him in a confidential manner. The sombre, darkening afternoon and the beginnings of rain on the coach windows seemed to have been specially arranged as a suitable background for his words.

'Well,' he said 'it's only a game, o' course. But things like Yolus an' Pozzidon, you can think of 'em almost as

if they was real. Sometimes in the winter, when we 'ave all them gales and bad weather and the waves get up rough and come all over the jetty, I sometimes think it's ol' Yolus and ol' Pozzidon out there in the sea, a long way out beyond Lundy Island, where it's deep and they've got plenty of room, blowin' about and 'eavin' 'emselves up and down, stirring it all up. You know why they do it? It's because they're sick of 'aving nobody think they're real any more. So they makes a great smite, beatin' an' blowin' about, all in a rage at their bein' forgotten for so long. I bet you think that's daft, don't you?'

'No, not at all,' said Mr. Stringston. 'I like it. You ought to write down things like that, Derry. That's a kind of poetry, you know. Like *Kubla Khan*.'

Derry didn't reply at once; then he said, rather awkwardly, as though the whole idea now made him uncomfortable: 'Oh, no, Mr. Stringston, I don't think I'd like doin' that. Things like that looks silly when they're wrote. My friends'd think I was potty if I even told 'em.'

So there they left the subject. Mr. Stringston had to admit to himself that Derry was probably right. It was a silly idea to put to a boy in his position. Still, it bothered him. He felt he ought to do something about Derry, that Derry was an imaginative boy, that if only he'd had the chance to stay longer at school who knows what he might not have done, how much better his chances for the future might have become? It even bothered him a little to see that Derry was obviously so very happy as a stable-boy. When Christmas came, before he went home, he gave Derry a book called *Tales From Homer*, hoping it might help to keep the lamps of Yolus and Pozzidon alight in an alien land. Derry thanked him politely as ever, but whether he ever read the book Mr. Stringston couldn't be sure.

CHAPTER THREE

ON THURSDAY 12th January 1899, soon after midday, Old Pozzidon awoke in the depths of the sea beyond Lundy Island, and he roused himself up to the surface and called out in a great voice to Yolus in the sky:

'Brother Yolus! The time hath come round once more to give 'em all a smite! Get out thy wind-bags and begin!'

And he started to heave himself up and down in the deep sea and blow it in great spouts out of his mouth.

At 1.30 that afternoon coastguards reported bad weather blowing up in the Bristol Channel. By 2 o'clock there were high winds and torrents of rain over the whole area. Hotels on the sea-front at Ilfracombe had their doors and windows beaten in by enormous waves. A high tide on the river Avon, the highest on record, flooded the port and the pier railway station at Bristol, and passengers had to be taken from the trains in boats. Boats in the harbour at Watchet were torn from their moorings, flung against each other and sunk. The sea wall there was washed away and the tide flooded the town.

The storm spread rapidly to all parts of the country. In Manchester and Birmingham people were killed by flying slates, by collapsing walls and falling chimneys. A Somerset newspaper reported seeing 'the lead on house-roofs curled up like straw ropes by the force of the wind'. A tented hospital which had been put up in Bromsgrove to deal with a fever epidemic was blown clean away. A church steeple was blown down in Reading. Everywhere there were reports of trees falling across railway lines in the paths of oncoming trains, and at one place on the Welsh coast where the line had been suddenly washed away, an entire goods train plunged down the embankment into the sea.

It was in the early afternoon of this same day, before anyone could guess they were in for one of the biggest storms of a lifetime, that the three-masted full-rigged ship *Forest Hall*, of 1900 tons register, was towed out of Bristol docks on her way to Liverpool. She was travelling in ballast with only a skeleton crew of fifteen. Her master, Captain James Uliss was to take on a full crew and cargo at Liverpool. She was now in tow to the tug-boat *J. Joliffe*, which was to take her down the Bristol Channel as far as St. David's Head, where she would set her sails and cast off.

But as the afternoon wore on, with the gale and the waves increasing in force every minute, it became doubtful whether the ship could be handled with such a small crew in such weather. It soon became doubtful even if they could tow as far as St. David's Head. Captain Uliss tried to signal the tug to change course and make for shelter in Carmarthen Bay on the Welsh coast. But because of the rough sea they were towing on a long cable, and in the heavy rain and flying spray, and with all the smoke blowing back from the tug's smoke-stack, and with the plunging of the waves, the two ships could barely see each other for much of the time. But Captain Uliss was thankful to see that the master of the tug evidently shared his misgivings, and was on his own initiative altering course towards the shelter of the Welsh coast. Then as they came around there was a sudden opposed pull of wind and sea, the cable lifted its length clear of the waves for a moment, tautened, strained, and broke apart. The *Forest Hall* yawed around broadside to the sea. The tug at once came about to try to recover her.

Captain Uliss quickly ordered to set two jibs and the spanker. This gave him just enough control over his vessel to bring her head round into the wind and hold her there while the tug came in as near as she dared, to try and take another line aboard. But try how they would for nearly an hour, with such huge seas running and in such a wind, all their efforts were in vain. Captain Uliss therefore at last signalled the tug to stand off, and sent men aloft to set the foresail. He was going to make for the anchorage on his own. Seeing this, the master of the tug was glad enough to turn about and make away back towards Bristol with the weather behind him, and very shortly the tug was lost to view in the rain and spray.

But she was hardly out of sight when the *Forest Hall* was struck suddenly by a wave of such force that the wheel was knocked spinning from the steersman's hand and the man was flung to the deck.

'Get two men on that wheel!' shouted the captain, and himself ran to steady it while the steersman picked himself up. Another wave of equal violence struck the ship broadsides and poured across the main deck. The captain and the steersman together pulled on the wheel to bring

the ship back on course. The wheel turned like a windmill in their hands and the ship didn't answer it.

'By God! She's broken her rudder!' said the captain, and then, at once: 'Call all hands, Mr. Mate! Strike all sail and let go both anchors! Move, man!'

Until the anchors were down the ship rolled and wallowed in the waves, out of all control. The anchors then steadied her. Pulling on them, her head came round again into the wind. But the advantage didn't last for long. It presently became all too certain that the anchors were dragging. The coast of Wales became more distant, and soon it was lost behind the curtains of dense rain and the seething grey waves.

All the afternoon the ship dragged her anchors back up-Channel going steadily further and further across towards the rocky Devonshire coast. Sometimes the anchors would seem to hold for a while. The ship would then steady herself. The waves would beat and break over her. Then she would reel around and go away again, once more dragging her anchors, out of control.

It was growing towards evening. As the day darkened the crew of the *Forest Hall* could see, now on one quarter, now on the other, as the ship alternately yawed and steadied, the vast escarpment of the Exmoor coast, with cliffs eight hundred feet high.

Captain Uliss was hoping against hope that in the now

shallower coastal water his anchors would at last take firm hold of the bottom, somewhere where he could ride out the storm. Visibility during the afternoon had been so bad that even had he flown distress signals they could not have been seen. At least with the coming darkness he could fire rockets, which would have a chance of being seen. There was not much consolation in that however. The huge black cliffs dragged and lurched slowly along, coming ever nearer towards him, in their curtains of flying spray. The direction of the wind was such that the ship was now dragging slowly along on a course parallel with the cliffs. Captain Uliss reckoned they might perhaps avoid being driven in onto them. But if so, they could hardly avoid going ashore in Porlock Bay. As darkness fell he could see tiny distant lights in houses safe on land. He gloomily looked his own situation in the face, and saw now there was little hope left of saving his ship. It only remained to try to save the crew.

'Are the rockets ready set, Mr. Mate?' he asked.

'Set and ready, Captain,' answered the Mate.

At 6.25 that evening Mr. Tom Pollard, the landlord of the Anchor Hotel at Porlock Weir, which is the village on the coast a mile and a half from Porlock Town, was going about stuffing wedges of paper in his tap-room windows to stop them rattling in the gale. He had had to bolt the outer door, to stop it being continually blown open. He reckoned it made little difference, as no one was likely to come in on such a dreadful night. But he was wrong. There came a banging at the door, and when he opened it there were two neighbours who lived up above on the cliff, both out of breath from running, and wet through. They said there was a large vessel out at sea, sending up distress signals. They guessed she couldn't be more than two miles out, and she appeared to be drifting inshore. There wasn't any doubt about it, the signals were being repeated and they'd both seen them.

They had come to the Anchor because Mr. Pollard operated a telegraph station from there to the main post-office in Porlock. It was a simple morse apparatus, set up in his little back office. They all three crowded in while he buzzed through to Porlock. It was almost a minute before there was any response; but then the answering buzz came, and he tapped out his message.

In the days of sail, the life-boat to call to a vessel in distress would always be the one nearest the incident on the windward side. In the present case this was the Lynmouth boat, twelve miles away. The Porlock postmaster therefore at once telegraphed the Lynmouth post-office as follows:

URGENT LIFEBOAT LARGE VESSEL DISTRESS
OFFSHORE PORLOCK TIME 6.33 PM URGENT

Mr. Ted Pedding, the Lynmouth postmaster, scribbled down the message while his wife Mary brought him his coat. He ran out into the little street where the wind nearly bowled him off his feet. Signalman Dick Morley's house was only a hundred yards away, but by the time he got there he was wet to the skin. He banged on the door. In the half-minute he waited there he saw waves like mountains breaking over the harbour wall. Dick Morley unbolted the door, let him in and read the message.

'Right, Ted', said he.

Two minutes later the first signal rocket surged up and exploded over Lynmouth.

CHAPTER FOUR

DERRY LARKINS had just come home from the stables and had hardly hung up his wet cap and coat when he heard the rocket go off. He saw his mother stop and listen a moment. Then she went on laying the table as if nothing was happening outside. Peeping through the curtains Derry saw Billy Pritchard running down the lane as fast as he could in his oilskins, towards the boat-house. He wanted to follow, to watch the launching. But he knew his mother, left alone, would be thinking of another storm and her own drowned sailorman, his father, six years ago. So they both went on pretending nothing was happening, and Derry sat down to his supper.

But then there was a knock at the door and Mrs. Pritchard came hurrying in, all tousled from the wind and rain, even coming from only next door. She said Billy had run off in such a hurry he had left his muffler behind. He would be sure to need his muffler: would Derry please run after him with it?

They all knew that Billy didn't and wouldn't want his muffler, but that an anxious mother wanted him to have it, for her anxiety's sake. But Derry jumped at the opportunity. 'Of course, Mrs. Pritchard,' he said, quickly pulling on his coat and cap. He took the muffler under his coat and ran off with it at once, leaving the two mothers to keep each other company. Besides, he knew Mr. Stringston would soon be in for his supper, and then everything would be all right.

It wasn't far to the boat-house, but the night was black as pitch, and Derry kept bumping into other people hurrying like him, without lanterns. Along the quay and in the narrow street there were lights from the windows, with people looking out, and down at the boat-house there were lanterns moving. Then Derry saw that these lights were all reflected in the water. In a minute he was himself nearly up to his ankles. The high tide was being met in the harbour by the swollen torrent of the Lyn, and the waves breaking over the sea wall were adding to the flood, and flooding the road. Even in the darkness one could see the white foam of those waves bursting against the jetty. They broke spouting upwards like the grey ghosts of huge trees, dwarfing the little watch-tower on the jetty beneath them, whose light they had put out. They hung in the air for a moment, then smothered down onto the roadway in a pelt of spray, hard as hailstones. Derry suddenly realised that if the life-boat were to be launched at all that night, it would have to be launched into the teeth and bellies of these monsters.

At the boat-house the boat was already being hauled out onto the flooded roadway by the crew and a gathering crowd who had come to help with the launch. In their black oilskins and sou'westers, and all bulked out with their life-jackets, it was difficult in the lanterned darkness to pick out one life-boatman from another; but Derry at last found Billy Pritchard and gave him the muffler.

Billy laughed. 'Anyway, young 'un,' he said, 'it don't look much like I'll need it. We can't launch. Well,' he said, pointing towards the pounding waves, 'look at that! 'Ow can we?!'

A wave even bigger than the others foamed upwards at the harbour wall and blotted out everything for a moment as it fell.

Coxswain Jack Crockham and George Pritchard were standing together, away from the others, further along the quay towards the pelting spray. They were joined by Mr. Oakley, the vicar, looking very odd in a borrowed sou' wester and sea boots with his spectacles and clergyman's collar.

' 'Tis hopeless, Vicar,' the Coxswain said, turning to him as he came up. 'There ain't a crew in the service as could launch in that. They'll have to call a boat from a more sheltered station, sir. I'm sorry.'

'I can see it's quite impossible, Jack,' said the Vicar. 'Come on then, we must telegraph Porlock at once.'

They hurried back to the post-office in the Street. Ted Pedding was there waiting.

'Quickly, Ted,' said the Coxswain, 'get Porlock. They must call another boat. We can't do it from here.'

While the postmaster was getting through, the Vicar was writing out the message. Coxswain Crockham said the life-boats at Watchet or Ilfracombe would both be able to launch, even on a night like this. But it was the devil of a long sail from Ilfracombe, and Watchet was down-wind from the wreck, so either boat would take a long time to make the rescue. However, it was the best that could be done. Meanwhile Ted Pedding was pressing down on the morse key, and frowning.

'I can't get anything,' he said.

They stared at him. He rattled the key up and down.

'I can't get anything,' he said again. 'It's dead,' he said. 'Vicar, the line's gone dead. I can't get through.'

The little post-office was now crowded to the door with storm-clad boatmen, all silent. The single oil lamp cast a sad light on their wet oilskins, cast big shadows around the walls. Under the lamp sat Ted Pedding, tapping at the useless key. He fiddled with the terminals. Then he gave up and turned to the silent faces watching him.

'The lines must have blown down, up over the moor,' he said. 'I can't do anything. I'm sorry.'

It was as he had said. During the short time since the message had come through from Porlock the telegraph lines over Exmoor had been torn away by the wind. All telegraph communication with other life-boat stations went through the Porlock exchange, which was now completely cut off from Lynmouth. To send a messenger over the moor on such a night would take many hours. A rider could hardly find his way at more than walking pace in the darkness. He might even never arrive. The moor was full of bogs and pitfalls. If he did arrive at last, only then could a telegram be sent to a distant life-boat station, assuming that these lines also had not blown down. The whole night would pass without help for the wreck.

In the Lynmouth post-office the wind howled down the chimney and rattled the windows. Only those nearest him could hear the voice of Mr. Oakley, as he said quietly:

'God help them, then, the poor fellows. No life-boat will get to them. The duty's ours, and nobody knows, except ourselves here, that we cannot fulfil it.'

But Coxswain Jack Crockham suddenly said: 'Oh, no, Mr. Oakley, no, sir!' He was a plain-faced, chin-bearded, non-drinking, non-swearing, pious man. He held up a big forefinger in the lamplight. He looked for a moment as if he had been turned to stone in the parish church. He said: 'You're right, Vicar; the duty's ours. It's us or it's nobody. And it can't never be nobody, not in the life-boat service. Go we must.'

A babble of protesting voices started up but he cut them short with a wave of his hand, shouting above the noise: 'Yes I know, we can't launch from 'ere. That's certain. But the wreck ain't 'ere neither, it's at Porlock. It'll be just as quick as anything else to carry the life-boat overland to Porlock and launch 'er from there.' He turned to the Second Coxswain and put the question to him: 'George, 'ow long d'ye reckon it'd take?'

The proposal, however, was greeted by such an exclamation from all round the room that George Pritchard's answer could not at first be heard. But Jack Crockham called again for quiet and repeated: 'What d'ye think, George? How long 'ud it take?'

'Thirteen, fourteen miles to Porlock Weir,' said George. 'Five hours, walking by daylight. Longer by night. It's now nearly seven o'clock. We shouldn't get there till about two after midnight, at earliest. And then we'd still 'ave to get out to the ship. That's if she's still afloat', he added. 'But you're right, Jack. We'll just 'ave to do it, and make the best we can of it.'

Everybody in the room was talking at once, and all to the same effect—that it couldn't be done. Thirteen miles over the moor in such a storm as this, all the way along very narrow roads between high banks and stone walls . . . the carriage would never get through, it was too wide . . . and the hills were too steep for such a load . . . and what about Porlock Hill, they'd never get boat and carriage down that difficult winding slope, even if they could get it up Countisbury. What, take the life-boat up Countisbury? 'You're mad, Jack,' they said, 'You'll never get 'er up there, not in a thousand years.'

It was not the life-boat crew who said these things, whatever they may have thought, but the crowd of neighbours who had gathered in the post-office and round the door. The life-boatmen waited for Jack Crockham to decide. He shouted out, above the din:

'Listen 'ere a minute. Life-boat Regulations, Regulation Twelve: "If a wreck occur at such a distance from the station as to require the boat to be transported along the coast, the Coxswain to procure sufficient 'osses for the purpose, and to proceed with all dispatch to the scene of the wreck." That's what it says, ain't it, George?'

'That's right, Jack,' said George Pritchard. 'Word for word.'

'It don't say nothin' about Countisbury 'Ill, though, do it,' said a voice from the back.

'It says "sufficient 'osses for the purpose",' answered Jack Crockham. 'For Countisbury 'Ill we'll need rather more sufficient 'osses than usual, that's all. Any other difficulties we'll deal with when we gets to 'em. Mr. Oakley, sir,' he said, turning to the Vicar, 'you're the Hon. Sec., and I think I ought to 'ave your consent for this. I am proposin' now to take this life-boat with all dispatch to launch 'er at Porlock. Do I 'ave your consent, sir?'

'You certainly have, Jack,' said the Vicar. 'Do whatever you can, and God be with you all.'

Jack Crockham pushed his way to the door, shouting

for his crew and launchers to go back at once to the boat-house. Outside the door he bumped into Derry Larkins.

'The very lad!' said he. 'You're Mr. Jonas's boy, ain't you? Quickly, me lad, get up the 'ill and find Mr. Jonas and tell 'im I wants every single 'oss 'e can spare, every single one, boy, and to 'ave 'em down 'ere by the bridge outside Evans' 'Otel in 'alf an hour. Run! Go!'

As Derry ran off he heard the Coxswain shouting after him again: 'Every single 'oss 'e's got, in 'alf an hour!' Derry panted up the zig-zag path to Lynton, the steepest but quickest way, faster than he'd ever done it in his life. Right below him the waves were breaking their huge

heads against the sea wall. Pozzidon pounded the cliffs, Yolus yelled in the sky. Ladies and gentlemen in their comfortable Lynton houses, peeping out between the window curtains, wondered what could be happening down there in Lynmouth. There seemed to be so many lights and lanterns moving about—and in such weather! And that boy out there, running up the hill, shouldn't he be at home out of the rain? He'll catch his death of cold!

Derry banged on Mr. Jonas's house door and gave his message.

'Every horse I can spare?' said Mr. Jonas, 'He can have eighteen or twenty if he likes. He don't want all that lot, surely?'

'Yes 'e do, though,' said Derry. ' 'E's goin' to take the life-boat up Countisbury 'Ill.'

'Lord save him!' exclaimed Mr. Jonas. 'He must have gone clean out of his mind! All right then, Derry, you run round and fetch Tom Wills. I'll get things going in the stables.'

Tom Wills was Mr. Jonas's most experienced driver and he lived just around the corner. The other driver, Will Vellacombe, lived over the stables, as did the head ostler. Jack Crockham could hardly have expected, in fact, to get his horses in the quick half-hour he had demanded; and in fact he did not. But it was not very much longer than that before Tom Wills and Derry led the first horses down Lynmouth Hill towards the bridge.

CHAPTER FIVE

LYNMOUTH could not remember a night like it. More than half the village was out in the street with lanterns. All the lamp-and-candle-lit cottage windows framed the dark figures of people peering out. Not even the noise of the wind or the booming of the sea could drown out all the sound of talk and shouting up and down the street. Fortunately it had stopped raining for the time being.

The life-boat *Louisa* had been hauled round with her carriage onto the short stretch of level road outside Evans's Lyndale Hotel. From here she would have a straight run over the bridge and up the first slope of Countisbury Hill. The two pairs of shafts, so long unused in the boat-house, had already been fitted to the carriage by the time Tom Wills and Derry arrived from Lynton with the horses.

'More comin' down, Cox'n Jack, said Tom.' 'You'll need 'em too.' He looked up at the huge bulk of *Louisa* looming above them in the lantern-light. 'Still,' he said reassuringly, 'the 'osses'll manage the pull, all right. But dang me, Jack,' he added 'I don't like that 'ere carriage. She's as wide as a church. You'll never get 'er through some o' them roads up there. And you can't go off the road over the moor. It'll all be as soft as butter with all this rain. She'd go down to 'er axles.'

'We'll get 'er through, Tom,' said the Coxswain. 'Signalman Dick's going on ahead of us with an advance party to knock down gateposts and widen corners where the road's too narrow. We've got to get through some'ow, Tom, and get through we will.'

A life-boat Signalman does not go in the boat. His duty is to follow the boat and keep contact with it by sight or signal from the shore. So Signalman Dick Morley was a fitting person to be in charge of the advance party on this occasion. Besides which he owned a horse and cart. With this and half-a-dozen volunteers he now came along the road and stopped for a last word with the Coxswain before setting off. In the cart were pick-axes, shovels, crowbars, sledge-hammers, spare lamps, drums of paraffin, the signalling equipment and all other gear not carried in the boat.

'Did you load the skids on?' asked the Coxswain.

The skids were lengths of flat wooden board which were kept for manhandling the boat over rough ground or on soft beaches where the carriage could not be used.

'There's a dozen or more,' said Dick Morley. 'I put 'em all in. You never know, we might need 'em. Right, Jack, I'll be off.'

It was half-past seven when the advance party moved off up the hill; and at the same time the remainder of the horses were coming down from Jonas's stables in Lynton, brought by Will Vellacombe, two ostlers, and Mr. Jonas himself.

'Lord have mercy on us,' he said, when he saw the size

of *Louisa* on the road. 'How many horses d'you reckon you'll need to get all that up the hill, Tom?'

'Every one we've got, guv'nor', answered the driver. 'I ain't taking no chances. But if we can get 'em all to pull together it'll be a miracle. Come on, then, lads, team 'em up. Quiet 'uns for leaders and wheelers, frisky 'uns in the middle. Mind that there Margie, she's been vexy all day.'

There were eighteen horses altogether, and all were now hitched in pairs to the boat-carriage. There were Daisy and Ben in the shafts, Busko and Lady as leaders, the difficult Margie tossing her head and stamping in the number three traces on the off-side. There were Grace and Charcoal and Jake, Sailor and Samson, Betty and Barnstable, Sue, Alice, Beauty, Stamper, Molly and Tomboy. Including the length of the boat, the whole train was nearly one hundred and thirty feet long, and stretched all along the road outside Evans's Hotel and across the bridge to the foot of the hill. It was a sight to be seen, and nearly all the people of Lynmouth on that cold and stormy night were out in the road to see it. To make it the more strange, the scene was all lit by the flickering light of paraffin flares blowing in the wind. The lights and shadows were leaping and dancing, the horses were all shifting and stamping and shaking their bridles. Lanterns were being taken up the hill to mark the seaward edge of the narrow road in the black darkness beyond. Jack Crockham mustered his crew and his launchers.

The launching party was made up of some of the regular life-boatmen who had not reached the boat-house in time to get the jackets that night, and of sturdy neighbours who knew the job, and knew the beach at Porlock Weir where they hoped to effect the launch. Among them were the landlord and barman from the Rising Sun, and the postmaster, Ted Pedding. The postmaster reckoned that since the storm had made an end of the telegraph for the time being, there was nothing at the post office that his wife couldn't attend to for the few hours he would be away. Besides which, he was the local agent for Lloyd's shipping insurance, and so he told himself it was his duty to go to the scene of the wreck in person. With the breakdown of the telegraph he couldn't get his necessary information any other way. He proposed going out in the life-boat if the Coxswain would let him.

'After all, Jack,' said he, 'in a way you could say it was me who started all this; so I might as well be there at the finish of it, eh?'

The Coxswain answered with a grin: 'You may feel a bit different when you get to t'other end, Ted. What, you, sittin' there in your little ol' post office all day? You ain't fit. I'll be surprised if you've even got enough breath to get up the 'ill.'

Ted laughed. 'Me?' he said, 'I've got enough to blow it down.' He was a big man and fit as a fiddle, and nobody knew it better than Jack Crockham. So Ted sent a message to his wife not to expect him back before the crew got home.

The crew that night, besides Coxswain Crockham and Second Cox George Pritchard were these men; Dick Vidler the Bowman, and his brother Jack; Jack Crockham's brother Dave; Jack Lord, the Cape Horner; Tom Tugsley, Dick Burrage and Charlie Craik; Bill Purvis, known as 'Limeburner' Purvis, because he was foreman at the lime-kiln nearby; Bert Bonnicott the postman; George Saul; and young Billy Pritchard on his first service.

'Well, young 'un,' said Billy to Derry as they stood together in the light of the flares, 'wish us luck.'

'But I'm comin' too,' said Derry. 'I'm comin' with the 'osses, ain't I?'

'Best ask yer mam first,' said Billy.

Derry was stung by this. 'I'm needed 'ere,' he said, and as if to echo him, Tom Wills suddenly called out:

'Hey, young Derry! Ask yer mam to let ye come up to the top o' the 'ill. We need 'elp with that Margie. She takes to you, don't she?'

'Yes she do, Mr. Wills,' Derry shouted back. 'I'll *tell* me mam!'

‘ ’Urry, then!’

He turned to run home, but met his mother in the road coming to look for him.

‘Up Countisbury!’ she said, ‘Oh Derry, be careful then. Keep away from the edge. Are you warmly wrapped?’

He was, as it happened. Then Mr. Stringston’s voice said:

‘Don’t worry, Mrs. Larkins. I’m going up, too. I’ll keep an eye on him.’

Nearly all the men and half the women in the village were going up, it seemed. They were going so that if need arose they could put their shoulders to the wheel or haul on the drag-ropes, and there was need for any number of lamps and carriers. Or if for no other reason, simply to follow such a strange and never-to-be-forgotten procession was reason enough to brave the weather, even in such a storm as this.

Coxswain Jack looked at his watch in the light of the flares. It was five minutes to eight. ‘Time we was off, Tom,’ he shouted. ‘You ready?’ Tom and the horses were all ready. Derry was holding Margie’s bridle, to steady her down. She was harnessed behind Charcoal, who was a quiet horse and would set a good example. ‘Off we go, then,’ shouted the Coxswain. Tom Wills cracked his whip, and Will Vellacombe with the lead horses Busko and Lady urged them forward.

But then everything went wrong. The horses, as Tom Wills had feared, being unused to such a long train, would not pull together. The shouting and the crowds and the whip-cracking upset them, they pulled aside, they pulled back. Even the drivers were shouting against each other. And when they at last all got moving the life-boat carriage came at a crooked angle onto the narrow bridge and jammed its wheel against the parapet. It was several minutes before they had everything straightened out again and started at last in good order, the horses now pulling together up the hill. It was five past eight, just one hour and thirty-two minutes since the call for help had come through from Porlock.

The beginning of the ascent was the steepest part, and it went up through a tunnel of trees. It was pitch dark, the way marked only by a line of lanterns. Ahead of the boat the long train of horses hauled up the rough muddy narrow road, with jingling and snorting, with the shouts of the drivers—*G'wern oop, there, Beauty!; Gee oop, Moll! Giddap, Stamper!* The lamps glimmered on the big flanks of the life-boat which filled the tunnelled space, sometimes almost catching upon the branches overhead. She was hauled and hauled, lying canted back at the steep angle of the slope, her bows projecting down the hill.

'Lord help us, I hope them keel-chains hold,' said Tom Tugsley to Bert Bonnicott. He held his lantern over to make sure, and the chains looked secure enough. If they had not been, had they broken, the boat would have launched itself like a thunderbolt off the keelway and crashed down into the crowd following behind. 'Best keep 'em all back a bit, anyway,' said Bert; and they waved the followers to hold back until there was a space between them and the boat labouring so steeply up the hill.

After fifteen minutes of steep going the slope of the hill became less severe; but now it emerged from the shelter of the trees and was exposed at last to the full violence of the storm. Down in the shelter of Lynmouth it had been bad enough; but up here on the hillside all

protection was gone. The gale bellowed and screamed, carrying upwards the salt spray from the waves breaking against the cliffs below; and now that it had its victims all out in the open on the climbing road, it began once more to pour out all the rain in the sky upon them. They all plodded on upwards, the horses, the boat, the boatmen, the village people; and their lanterns made a thin twinkling thread of dim light on the side of the black hill. The difficulty now was to keep the lanterns from blowing out.

The road now became very narrow. It had been built by hacking away the rock on the side of the hill, which now formed a high jagged wall on the inland side. On

the other side, lumps of the rock had been used to form a low barrier wall between the road and the grass slope which ran down to the cliff edge. At the narrowest places Dick Morley and his advance party had knocked away some of this wall, to make wheel-room for the carriage. The passage at these places was tricky, but they managed it with lamps along the edge. All the way up, by keeping the carriage as far over as they could from the cliff edge on one side, they had trouble with the wheel hubs grinding against the rock face on the other. Sometimes they jammed, and then the whole procession had to stop. It was slow going.

Derry found himself penned in a narrow passage between the horses and the rock face, but this had the advantage that the horses kept the wind and rain off him. Fortunately Margie was behaving herself. She plodded on pulling her weight, much encouraged by Derry's occasional chat: 'Goo-ern there, Margie girl, goo-ern!'

Mr. Stringston was following with the launchers a little way back down the road. When they came out from the protection of the trees, and the storm grew so fierce some of the villagers had turned back, and for a moment Mr. Stringston had been tempted to do the same. But he remembered he had promised to keep an eye on Derry to the top (not that he could see him now at all); and, besides, a sudden sense of the drama of it all had taken hold of him. The howling storm, the precipice, the labouring boat, the gaunt men and their lanterns, how grand it all was! He himself was well and warmly clad, with a thick jersey under his mackintosh, with good boots and leather gaiters, and a deerstalker hat with the flaps tied down over his ears. He was carrying his rough-cut ash walking stick upon his shoulder. It cannot truly be said that he made a heroic figure; but at that moment he felt himself heroic. He, even he, Alfred Nathaniel Stringston, had been there in person on the night they took the life-boat up Countisbury Hill in the great storm of 1899. He would be with them still when they gained the summit, which even now was not far off. It was indeed a heroic night!

And it chanced that as these men were labouring with

their boat to the summit of the great hill, the god Yolus espied them there from above, and he called out to Pozzidon below in Porlock Bay:

'Brother Pozzidon! Behold the rescue boat upon the hill! Look sharp with thy games in the bay there, or thee'll be too late!'

Then old Pozzidon looked back over his shoulder and said:

'Oho, yes, I sees 'em! Boats on wheels, that's saucy! I'll give 'em wheels! Watch this!' And he stretched forth his finger in the dark.

The carriage and boat tipped suddenly forward and lurched to one side against the rock-face. The horses pulled crooked in their traces, stamping and slithering in the mud, and all came to a halt upon the hill.

CHAPTER SIX

EVERYTHING was a muddle of cold mud, rain, wind and cross-purposes. Half the lanterns had blown out. Everybody was shouting at once, either to mind out, or to go here, or do that, or simply to know what the matter was.

Tom Tugsley, who had been marching on the inside between the boat and the rock-face, had barely managed to jump back out of the way as the carriage slumped round and lurched into the rock beside him. At the same time a four-foot wheel, all on its own, rolled back past him down the hill and fell over against the wall a few feet away.

'Look out!' he shouted. 'There's a wheel off! Quick, get them scotches under!'

They put scotches under all three remaining wheels to stop the carriage rolling its great load back down the hill. Then they brought their lanterns round to inspect the trouble.

It was the front offside wheel which from its continual jamming and bumping against the rock wall, in the dark on the narrow road, had loosened and lost its lynch-pin, and so worked its way off the axle. Fortunately neither the wheel nor the axle had suffered damage as they came apart.

Spare lynch-pins were carried in the tool box. All they had to do was to find one, up there in the boat, in the rain, in the dark, in the wind, in the flickering lantern light.

'Danged thing's blown out again,' shouted Tom Tugsley from up in the boat. They handed him up another lantern, and presently a spare lynch-pin was found, and the tools and jacks passed down.

What they had now to do was to get the horses out of the shafts, jack up the keelway and the fore-carriage, get the wheel back on its axle, fit the spare lynch-pin, let down the jacks, bring the horses back into the shafts, and there they would be, ready to move on again. They had plenty of helping hands, and in the ordinary way it might not have taken very long. But they were exposed on the most bare and open part of the road, at the top of the hill. The wind and rain beat upon them with an outrageous ferocity. They were already wet to the skin. The darkness was intense. Their lanterns were continually blowing out, and were difficult to re-light. Working as fast as they could under these circumstances it took them nearly forty minutes from the time the wheel came off till they were ready for the road again.

Meanwhile most of the villagers who had come to carry lights and to haul and push the carriage on the hill, if this had been needed, had decided there was nothing more they could now do except go home and dry out their clothes. There remained about twenty, including Mr. Jonas's drivers and ostlers, the postmaster Ted Pedding, and Mr. Stringston, who was looking for Derry. He presently found him sheltering with Billy Pritchard in the lee of Margie's flank, and trying to keep her quiet.

She was growing vexy again, and small wonder. The poor horses were streaming with wet and weather, standing still in the bitter wind.

'We'd best be getting back down now, Derry,' said Mr. Stringston. 'We've reached the top, and the wheel will be on in a few minutes. If you don't leave now you might have to go all the way to Porlock.'

'That's it, young 'un,' said Billy. 'Back to yer mam.'

'But this ain't the top, Mr. Stringston,' said Derry. 'Blue Ball's the top. I got to go up that far, anyway. I said I would.'

The Blue Ball is a little country inn just over the summit of Countisbury Hill. It stands in a slight hollow between the crest of the road and the open moor beyond. Exposed as it is, it was a place of shelter compared with the hillside road above the cliffs that night. A number of the helpers who found themselves with nothing to do while the wheel was being put on, had gone on ahead to warm themselves by the tap-room fire while they had the chance. Dick Morley and the advance party had been in there briefly an hour before, so Fred Luscombe the innkeeper already knew what was on the way.

It was twenty minutes to ten by Jack Crockham's watch when the wheel was back on again and the horses back in the shafts. Life-boat *Louisa* moved off once more to the crest of the hill. Five minutes later she halted outside the Blue Ball. So far so good, Jack Crockham said to himself. He had overcome the worst of his obstacles, or so he thought. Now all that remained was the ten-mile stretch of open moor between Countisbury and Porlock. But with the wheel coming off he had lost valuable time, and he had none to spare. He had quickly to form up his column of march, and press on. Fred Luscombe the innkeeper, came out with a brandy bottle to offer a quick nip all round. 'Compliments of the 'ouse on a cold night, and good luck, Cox'n Jack,' said he.

'Thank 'ee kindly, Fred, for the others, but not for Dave and me,' said Coxswain Jack. 'Us Crockhams never touches it, ye know.'

'We all knows about you Crockhams,' said the landlord, 'so this 'ere jug's for you. 'Ot cocoa.'

'Nothin' in it, you sure?' asked Dave, sniffing it suspiciously.

'Nothin',' said the landlord. 'Just cocoa—'ot.'

'Thankee, then, Fred, and very welcome it is,' said the Coxswain. 'We're soaked to the skin, if ye must know.'

There was a mug of cocoa found for Derry Larkins also, and he gulped it down quickly while keeping well out of Mr. Stringston's sight. Derry was wet and cold, but no wetter or colder, he supposed, than any of the others. The hot cocoa had a powerfully ambitious effect upon him. If Yolus and Pozzidon had known more about the stimulating power of hot cocoa, they might have thought twice about taking on such people as Derry Larkins and Jack and Dave Crockham that night.

Mr. Stringston, however, was not quite of the same mind. His heroic mood had wilted a great deal while the wheel was being put on, and he had found the innkeeper's nip of brandy some help to its recovery. It occurred to him that he could do with a little more of the same before facing the long return walk down the empty, pitch-dark, wind-blasted hill with Derry. So he stepped for a brief two or three minutes into the candlelit tap-room out of the rain, and paid the potman for one more nip. Only small it was, but he found himself very satisfactorily unwilted by it, and well fitted once again to face the howling weather outside. The innkeeper had just come in and was peeling off his oilskins. Mr. Stringston pulled down his ear-flaps and tied the tapes firmly under his chin, he grasped his good ash-stick in his resolute hand, and with a hearty 'good-night, landlord!' strode heroically out of the door into the storm and the empty road. Empty because, unheard by him, the lifeboat with all its crew and helpers, and Derry Larkins, had already moved off onto the moor.

He stood for a full minute, which in such a storm was a long time to stand, not knowing which way to turn. On the one hand he had to make the long descent of Countis-

bury Hill, with at the end of it the shameful confession to Mrs. Larkins that he had allowed Derry to go off over the moor to catch his death of cold while he, the self-appointed guardian angel, had been swigging brandy in the Blue Ball; or, on the other, he had to go over the moor after the life-boat and get hold of Derry and try to turn him about while there was still time before they had all gone too far. Of the two, he at last thought the latter the less disagreeable choice, and so he set off after the life-boat, still going uphill a little way till the road levelled out on the open upland of Countisbury Common. Here he was a thousand feet above sea level, and exposed once more to the full force of the streaming gale.

The road was hard to follow in the darkness. There was no sign of the boat company with its lanterns ahead, because the road was going around the side of the hill at the summit of Countisbury Common. Mr. Stringston groped and stumbled his way along very slowly, bumping into the roadside wall first on one side, then on the other, seeing nothing anywhere. He had gone about half a mile and was on the point of giving up the pursuit and groping his way back again to the Blue Ball when he came round a corner and saw the lights of the life-boat company dimly flickering, some distance ahead. Encouraged by this he stepped out to increase his speed, and at once caught his foot in a rut in the road, and fell, soaking his sleeve in a puddle. Wet and muddy, but still assisted by some of the valiance he had obtained at the inn, he pressed on, and was at last rewarded. The life-boat had been brought briefly to a halt at the passage of a narrow corner of the road, and before she could move on again Mr. Stringston had caught up with her.

Dick Morley's advance party had had to work hard

widening the corner. They had knocked down the dry-stone wall on one side, and used it to fill in the roadside ditch. The corner was thus made passable, but only just, for it was very rough and the stones under the heavy wheels kept sinking into the soft bottom of the ditch, and the helpers had to keep filling in on top with more loose stone; besides which, being on a corner the horses couldn't get a long straight pull at the carriage, and it had to be pushed by the crew the last few yards till it was safely around. So while all this was going on Mr. Stringston came up and put his hand on Derry's shoulder, and said as firmly as he could:

'Derry, you know you shouldn't be here. You're not a man yet, whatever you may think. Your mother will be worrying herself to death. Come on back now, for goodness' sake.'

'I'm thirteen, Mr. Stringston, I ain't a baby', Derry replied, in a voice that was in fact much more firm than Mr. Stringston had been able to manage. 'I'm old enough to work, ain't I? 'Ere I am, not even a bit tired. Now I come so far I can't go back. I got to go on to Porlock with the others.'

'See now, Derry,' said Mr. Stringston, 'if you go on to Porlock, so must I. I promised your mother I'd keep an eye on you. And I've got a long day's work to do at the school tomorrow. You're putting me in a very difficult position.'

'It ain't fair of you to put it to me like that, Mr. Stringston,' said Derry, 'and you know it ain't.'

It wasn't, and he did know it. Moreover, it was a tactical mistake. It had been a weak appeal, and Derry had rejected it. Mr. Stringston felt himself morally defeated at one blow.

Meanwhile, the boat had been eased around the corner and was moving off again with all her company. The wind over the moor howled all around them, blowing out the lanterns. Yolus was making a holiday of it. At one time all the lanterns blew out but two, and the march was held up for five minutes relighting them, before they could see their way along.

Derry and Mr. Stringston were marching together in the rear of the procession. Mr. Stringston felt he couldn't leave Derry. Derry couldn't go forward as he would have liked, to pick up with Margie again and keep her quiet (not that she needed it; the weather had been more than a match for her vexation). Then all of a sudden Derry felt that Mr. Stringston needed sympathetic handling almost as much as Margie did. Here was the schoolmaster trudging along with his walking-stick and the rain running down off the peak of his deerstalker hat, looking very gloomy, while Derry was feeling splendidly cheerful. He found himself saying in a buoyant voice:

'Never mind the rain, Mr. Stringston! Just think what a fine thing this is to be doin'! Think of all them old 'Omer 'eroes in the book you gave me, Christmas. Ain't this just what they would do? What about that ol' Ajax, eh? 'Im standin' up there on that rock, stickin' 'is chest out and defyin' the gods: "Dang you, Yolus and Pozzidon, you can't do nothin' to me!" That ain't very different from us, is it?'

'You must mind your language, Derry,' said Mr. Stringston, rather tartly. 'Besides, Pozzi'—he corrected himself quickly—'Poseidon got the better of Ajax. He split the rock Ajax was standing on; he split it with his trident. And that was the end of Ajax. He was drowned.' Mr. Stringston felt a little better, having scored one up on this point of scholarship. Derry however, fenced back quickly, parried the point, and changed the rules of the game.

'Ah, but that was *then*,' he said. 'That ain't *now*. It'll be different now, with old Jack Crockham. You'll see. The 'Ell with Pozzidon!'

Outplayed once more Mr. Stringston didn't even feel able to expostulate about the language. Meanwhile, Pozzidon, nettled, had decided to take a hand again on his own account. He was all in favour of human conformity and respectfulness and of keeping the rebels in order; and he had a good trick to play. It was a trick called Ashton Lane.

CHAPTER SEVEN

AT LEAST the rain had stopped again. They all trudged on, making a better pace in better spirits, their lanterns all swinging. They followed the road round the side of Kipscombe Hill, and then they saw lights ahead of them. It was Dick Morley and the road party. They had widened the road around another sharp corner and taken down a length of wall beyond it. Further along they had dug down two gateposts; and then they had come to the beginning of Ashton Lane. They had all feared that this would be the worst part of the road, and so it was, every inch of it.

George Pritchard was marching at the head of the column, and he came up with Dick standing there in the road waiting for them. They all came to a halt.

'Hullo, Dick,' said George. 'Trouble?'

'Take a look down there,' said Dick in reply, jerking a thumb over his shoulder to the lane beyond.

The road at Ashton Lane was not only narrower than elsewhere, but the walls were continuous all the way on both sides and for long stretches they were built along the top of high banks. Not anywhere was there room for the width of the carriage; in some places the lane was hardly wider than the boat itself. It was like this for a long mile. It was quite impossible to widen it. George Pritchard and Jack Crockham and Dick Vidler and Tom Wills went along down the lane with Signalman Morley and were away for nearly a quarter of an hour. They came back over the moor on the other side of the wall, to see if that way offered any possible detour. The moor was fairly firm and level at the far end of the mile, but there were bad boggy patches midway, and at the near end there were steep slopes. The weight of the boat on such muddy ground and with such a slope would make the carriage impossible to handle, nor could the horses hope to pull it. They all returned to the main party with glum faces. 'No luck, then, Jack?' asked Dave.

Then said Jack Crockham with what, for him was the nearest he would allow himself for an oath.

'Bust me, Dave,' he said, 'luck or no luck, we ain't brought this boat all this way for nothing! We ain't goin' to be turned back now! We'll get 'er through to Porlock if it takes us all night, bust me! We'll take the boat off the carriage and pull 'er through the lane on the skids. The carriage can go over the moor all right, unladen, and meet us at the other end. What d'ye think, boys? We might do it that way, mightn't we?'

'We can 'ave a dang good try at it, anyway,' said George Pritchard. Everyone agreed. As Cox'n Jack had said, they hadn't come all that way to be turned back now.

Jack Crockham held the lantern to his watch. It was ten past eleven. 'Come on, then, lads,' he said. 'We've no time to waste.'

The first thing was to get *Louisa* off her carriage. This presented a difficulty, as she was facing to the rear, and to take her along the road she would need to go bow first, not backwards against her rudder-post. She would have to be turned, and there was no room to turn her in the road. But there was a gateway on the south side, through which they intended to take the carriage. First, therefore, they dug and took away the gateposts to make the clearance wide enough for the carriage. They unhitched some of the horses, and with the rest brought the carriage round into the gateway, so that *Louisa*'s bows were towards the road. Then they jacked up the keelway (which gave them some difficulty at first because of the softness of the ground under the jack; but they made a base for it with stones from the wall) and drew away the fore-carriage. Then they lowered the jack and brought the front of the keelway gently down onto the ground. Then they released the keel-chains and drew the rear-carriage back across the road, letting *Louisa*'s keel down the keelway and steadying her on each side till she lay level on the ground. Then they manhandled her, a dozen men on each side, back round into the road facing the way she would go. When she was clear of the gateway they were then able to bring the hind-carriage through into the field and link it up again with the fore-carriage.

Next they began to separate the horses into two teams. They chose the ten quietest to pull the boat. The remaining eight they led off into the field and teamed up to the carriage. Tom Wills was in charge of this party, and he took Derry with him. 'What, thee still 'ere, young Derry,' he said, when he saw him. 'Thee ought to be at 'ome in bed, me lad. If thee was mine I wouldn't 'alf give 'ee a wallopin' for bein' out so late. Come on, then, git to them 'osses.'

Mr. Stringston was standing beside Dick Morley's cart

when young Billy Pritchard and Limeburner Purvis came and started unloading the skids, laying them at the side of the road. He found himself saying to them: 'Let me lend a hand.'

'Thank 'ee sir,' said Purvis, 'very good of 'ee, sir, I'm sure.'

Mr. Stringston put his walking stick in the cart and started to help with the skids. There were fifteen of these, each five feet six inches long, by eighteen inches wide. They were soon unloaded. What, Mr. Stringston wondered, had Purvis meant by saying it was 'good of him' to help. He hadn't come all this way for nothing, either. He was muddy and wet now like the rest of them. He took off his deerstalker hat and threw it along with his stick in the cart, and unbuttoned his mackintosh which he found cumbersome, though the wind was very cold.

They started to lay out the skids up the lane, with a six-foot gap between each. This made a pathway one hundred and sixty feet long. This meant that as the boat passed across the skids, each would have to be picked up and carried forward up the column thirty-two times. They would need all the hands they could get for it. Only a small party therefore went with the carriage, with shovels and pickaxes to deal with any obstacles in their way. The majority, about thirty in all, now that they had been joined by Dick Morley's party, stayed with the boat.

By the time all these things had been done, and a rigging had been made fast to *Louisa*'s bows to harness the horse team, and both parties were at last ready to set off on their separate ways, Jack Crockham's watch showed him it was already midnight. The storm was as fierce as ever, and it was beginning to rain again. The carriage party went off over the moor and its lamps were soon lost in the downpour. Jack Crockham passed the word up the line to Will Vellacombe at the head with the horses to move on; and off they all went into the lane.

They all of them thought, then and all their lives after, that this was by far the worst part of that night's journey. It was slow, muddy, wearying toil the whole way. To keep the boat's keel along the skids was in itself most

difficult, with only the poor light of the lanterns to see by. And the carrying of the skids from the rear to the front of the column as *Louisa* slithered her slow, uneasy way along was a labour that had frequently to be relieved by other helpers. Mr. Stringston, his clothes, face and hair all muddy and streaming with rain, found himself sometimes squeezing between the boat and the wall in a space so narrow that he could hardly manage to get through, carrying his skid. Once or twice indeed the lane became so narrow that *Louisa* only passed through with an inch to spare on each side. But they all scrambled along, slowly. 'Chin up, Billy,' said George Pritchard to his brother from time to time, 'we're nearly there.' It was the longest nearly ever, Billy thought.

'Mind the 'osses feet in them wires,' shouted Will Vellacombe from up ahead. A thin skein of wire lay right across the path. It was the broken telegraph line, the cause of all their trouble. They dragged *Louisa* across it, leaving it straggled behind them in the mud and stones.

Meanwhile out on the moor the carriage was making its way slowly along without much trouble. At one point, soon after they started off, having managed their way past the slopes, the party had to pick their way carefully round a boggy patch which Derry was the first to find, sinking in halfway to his knees. This was a bad moment, but having passed it they went on up a rise onto hard ground, and thereafter the only difficulty was to keep direction. It was very dark and still raining. Harry Lacey, one of the grooms, tripped and fell and ricked his ankle; but he said it wasn't bad, he could manage along. At the far end of their journey, when they at last reached the road again beyond the narrows of Ashton Lane, they found only a rotten old wall of loose stones to hinder them, which they easily cleared away, and so got the carriage through and onto the road once more.

Looking back down Ashton Lane at first they could not see anything, nor hear anything except the incessant howling of the wind. But in a little while they began to see lanterns moving in the distance. They watched the restless clusters of lights coming slowly on towards them, foot by foot, or even, it seemed, only inch by inch, sometimes halting altogether, then moving forward again. The lane towards the end had reached its very narrowest part, and at one point the skid-carriers could not get by along the boat at all, but had to pass the skids under it to those ahead, who took them on and laid them. Then at last the lane began to widen. There was room to manoeuvre, room to breathe. The end of the lane was in sight and the boat company could see the carriage company ahead, waiting for them. Their hearts warmed, their pace increased. And so, after another five minutes of hauling and labouring, the long line of rain-soaked horses and men, all so covered in mud they looked as if they were made of it, came with their glimmering lamps out of the narrows and onto the road, and brought the life-boat *Louisa* through, and halted her beside her carriage.

' 'Ullo, Tom,' said George Pritchard to Tom Wills. 'You got 'ere, then, I sees.'

'Yes, we got 'ere,' said Tom. 'What about you, any trouble?'

'No,' said George; 'only so long as we don't none of us never 'ave to do that agin so long as we live, no trouble at all.'

So they set to work all over again. They dismounted the keelway from the fore-carriage. They hauled *Louisa* up onto the keelway and fixed the chains. They jacked her up and brought back the fore-carriage. They brought back the horses and harnessed them. They were ready to move off. They moved off.

Coxswain Jack Crockham stayed behind in the road for a short minute, to attend to the needs of nature. Finding himself alone, he turned and looked back down the road towards Ashton Lane and solemnly thumbed his nose at it. Then he grinned, all alone there in the road.

'So much for you,' he shouted into the wind, addressing the darkness towards Ashton Lane, and all the elemental forces that might be lurking there. 'We said we'd do it, and what we said we'd do we done! You couldn't stop us. Remember that!'

It ceased raining at that very moment.

'That's better,' said the Coxswain to himself. 'Wore 'em down a bit, them old Elements. That's what we're 'ere for, after all, to get the better o' *them*!'

But it didn't do to be too boastful. As he caught up with his company again they were going round the hillside towards County Gate. Here, by day, for the first time since leaving Countisbury Hill, the high road is in full view of the sea. But on this dark night there was nothing to be seen down there, only a blackness full of howling wind. Somewhere out in that blackness in the sea there was a ship in distress. For what must have been the twentieth time Jack Crockham held the lantern to his watch. It was half past one. Seven hours had passed since the message had come from Porlock. In all this time they had completed no more than a third of their journey to the launching place.

CHAPTER EIGHT

THEY came to County Gate. They dug down one of the gate-posts, and passed through into Somerset.

The road here turned inland from the sea again. The going was easier. They had six men with lanterns going ahead of the leading horses, three on each side of the road, and with these as markers they were able to move along faster, making up a little of their lost time. The wind had eased off a little, so they could hear themselves talk. Billy Pritchard found himself marching next to Dick Vidler the Bowman, who was Billy's skipper in the working days. Dick was always a cheerful man.

' 'Lo, young Billy,' said he. 'Where you bin, eh? Ain't seen you around all night.'

'What you mean, skipper? I bin 'ere all the time.'

'Oho, yes, I bet you 'as. You bin up there in the boat, sleepin'. I knows you of old. Sleepin' in the boat. That's right, ain't it Bert? Eh, Charlie?'

Postman Bert Bonnicott knew very well how to pick up this game:

'Right? O' course it's right. Fast asleep in the boat under the life-jackets. I seen 'im up there.'

'And 'eard 'im,' added Charlie Craik. 'Snorin'. You

could 'ear 'im from one end of Ashton Lane to the other. Like my ol' pig.'

'That ain't true!' declared Billy. 'I don't never snore.'

'Oh come now, Billy,' said Dick 'you must do. Who else could it a' bin? You was the only one sleepin'.'

'You ask Limer Purvis,' shouted Billy, slightly annoyed, above their laughter. 'I bin workin' with 'im all the time, all up and down the lane. 'E'll tell you.'

'Ah, but Limer's got a dreadful bad memory for faces,' said Charlie. ' 'E'd never know who you was. You ain't never bin on a service before.'

'It won't do, Billy boy,' said Bert, very solemnly. 'Sleepin' on your first service. You'll never make a life-boatman, you won't.'

They went on chaffing him like this, marching along at a good pace, all the way over Yenworthy Common.

Marching at the head of the column Jack and Dave Crockham and George Pritchard and Tom Wills were discussing their next obstacle, the difficult descent of Porlock Hill.

'Steeper than Countisbury in places, and all them crinks and turns, Tom. Think you can manage it?' asked the Coxswain.

'Well, if I can't nobody can,' said Tom. 'I bin takin' the coaches up an' down Porlock ever since it were a tiny 'ill no bigger'n a loaf of bread. Mind you, though, this 'ere life-boat be the biggest thing as ever went down it, that's perfect certain.'

'If it ever do get down,' said Dave.

'Or if it don't get down too lightnin' quick,' said George. 'That's what I'm afeared of.'

'I'm only feared o' one thing,' said Tom, 'and that's

the ol' boat comin' off 'er carriage. With only them two keel-chains to 'old 'er on it, if the carriage turleys over a bit on one o' they sharp corners she may break off and go over broadsides. Or goin' down one o' the steep straights, she may lep off over the front and flatten out the poor 'osses like butter. But if you can keep 'er on the carriage, Jack, I can get 'er down the 'ill.'

They were approaching the shelter of the woods at Culbone. This was the only good shelter they would have between Lynmouth and Porlock Hill. They therefore decided to halt at Culbone stables and lash the boat securely to her carriage there. They also decided to leave some of the horses at the stables, since now they had no more steep hills to climb, but only to descend, and the eighteen horses they had with them were more difficult to manage than their work was worth. Twelve, said Tom, would now be enough for anything they were likely to meet.

'We can leave 'Arry Lacey be'ind with 'em, to take care of 'em till mornin' ' said Tom. ' 'E's turned 'is ankle, and it comin' up on 'im, so 'e can't walk much further. And young Derry Larkins, 'e'll be pretty glad to stop off by this time, poor little nipper. My fault, I suppose for callin' on 'im. I never meant 'im to come all this far, though.'

Derry overheard this. He had taken over the leading horse Busko's bridle from Will Vellacombe, and so was not far behind Tom Wills as he spoke, though hidden behind Busko's shoulder. Derry was certainly now very tired, and on any ordinary day or night would have been glad of any ordinary reason to escape from the toils of this adventure, out of his wet clothes and into bed. Perhaps if he had not overheard Tom Wills planning to set him aside at Culbone, if he had just been unexpectedly faced with the instruction to stay and look after the horses, he might have been glad to comply. But now he had time to reflect. Having come so far, as Cox'n Jack had said in Ashton Lane, he wasn't going to stand off now and miss the rest of the journey. He wasn't going to miss the descent of Porlock Hill. He wasn't a poor little nipper, he was thirteen, and earned his own wages.

They entered the woods, and shelter descended all round them like peace, the wind roaring over the tops of the trees above them, not touching the road. They pulled up outside Culbone stables and quickly set to work. While some were roping *Louisa* more securely onto the carriage, others, under Tom Wills' direction were separating the horses. They took out Samson, Molly, Sue, Tomboy, Jake and Margie. There was an old man living at the stables to mind the place for the winter, and he and Harry Lacey between them started rubbing the horses down and putting them in the stalls. Tom Wills shouted for Derry.

'Now what's 'appened to 'im I wonder,' he muttered, having received no reply. Mr. Stringston was hurrying past, carrying lanterns to Dick Morley's cart, which had followed them from Ashton Lane. It carried the spare paraffin, with all its other gear. All the lamps were by now beginning to burn low, and Mr. Stringston was glad to make himself useful, refilling them.

'Beg pardon, sir,' said Tom, catching his sleeve, 'You seen that young Derry anywheres? I wants 'im back 'ere to stay with the 'osses.'

'I saw him a moment ago, Tom. I'll tell him as soon as I find him.'

Tom thanked him and went back to his team. Mr.

Stringston as he moved round looked for Derry among the crew, who had soon finished lashing down the boat and were now tying off rope-ends and looping them back. 'I seen 'im up in the boat, not two minutes since', said Tom Tugsley, answering Mr. Stringston's inquiry. But before Mr. Stringston had time to seek further Jack Crockham had looked at his watch again and found it was ten minutes to three.

'All right, lads, stand away! Let's get movin'!' he shouted. The drivers cracked their whips and called to the horses: 'Giddap! G'yerp, there!' And the whole troop moved off once again with their lanterns into the darkness along the road.

Quickly, before following after, Mr. Stringston looked in at the stable door. 'Young Larkins in here?' he asked Harry Lacey.

'No, sir,' was the reply. 'Old Tom were lookin' fur 'im, not five minutes ago. But 'e didn't want to stay back 'ere. I knows that. 'E'll be up there along o' the boat, you may be sure.'

Mr. Stringston was indeed sure; and he was right. Derry had climbed into the boat with the others while they were making fast the lashings, and at the first opportunity, when the others had climbed out, he had hidden himself under the heap of the crew's life-jackets and oilskins which had been put there. When he heard Tom calling his name he was on the point of climbing down after all, to answer, and to be left behind on the comfortable straw in the stables; for his head was reeling with sleep. Whereupon he fell asleep, there and then. He awoke half an hour later, wet and cold in the boat, jolting along in the wind, once again out on the open moor.

For they had left the comfort of Culbone woods a long

mile behind them and had just now come over the top of Hawkcombe Head, the highest and most bleak part of their whole journey. Here was nothing but the high wind, howling again, now as harshly as ever, without even the lowest wall at the roadside to break it. The wild ponies out on the moor stood bunched together in the lee of whatever poor bits of shelter they could find. As *Louisa* and her hurrying troop went by down the slope towards Porlock, the swinging lanterns shone upon the eyes of sheep who, huddled in the ditches at the side of the road, struggled out in a fright and went bleating off into the dark.

At this high point the road overlooks Porlock Bay itself. From here the life-boat crew might have seen, had there been any, the lights of a ship. Had there been any, they might have seen rockets, flares, signals of distress. But they saw nothing. They wondered, indeed, if there could now be anything left afloat to see.

CHAPTER NINE

AT THE top of Porlock Hill they halted to put the safety-chains on the rear carriage wheels, and attach the drag-ropes. They also fitted the big iron shoes or skid pans under the wheels. Tom Wills and Will Vellacott led back eight of the horses to follow in the rear with Dick Morley's horse and cart, leaving only four in the carriage, to control it around the corners.

While all this was going on, Derry climbed down from the boat. He had hoped not to be seen, but the hope was vain.

'Ah!' said Tom Tugsley 'It was you, was it! We was wonderin' why it were such a 'eavy load. Passengers in the boat.'

'Why, young 'un,' said Billy. 'I'll wager you've bin fast asleep up there, all the time.'

'No, I ain't,' Derry said. 'Only but a minute or two.'

'Under the life-jackets, out of sight,' said Billy. 'You'll never make a life-boatman, you won't. Will 'e Charlie?'

'Not 'im,' echoed Charlie Craik. 'Snorin'. You could 'ear 'im all the way from 'ere to Culbone.'

It was useless to protest. Fortunately for Derry they

all now began to move off down the hill, and there was no more time or thought for bantering.

They had all the men possible on the drag-ropes. Mr. Stringston took his place between Dave Crockham and Ted Pedding, the postmaster. Those that weren't on the ropes carried lights. So they went down the steepening slope towards the tunnel of trees that shrouded the steepest gradients and the sharp turns. As the tunnel swallowed them down they felt the carriage beginning to pull away on its locked wheels. They all hauled back on the drag-ropes as it went into the steep, and they steadied it round the corner between the lanterns held to mark the sides of the road. Beyond, it was steeper still for a short distance. The locked wheels ploughed into the road, jolted against stones, struck sparks out from under the skid-pans. They hauled back, let her down gently. Now another curve, bending round to the right very sharply. This was the most dangerous place. Dick Morley had got three big flares going there, lighting up the tunnel of trees like a blacksmith's cavern. The road cambered steeply over around the bend. They steadied *Louisa* to a stop, then eased her very gently round.

'Nicely, nicely, lads,' called Tom Wills. 'Doin' it beautiful. Gently now.'

Gently round. And ahead of them a long very steep descent, straight for two hundred yards, and then (as they knew, but could not see in this dark) another sharp bend.

Down they went. The sparks shot out from the wheels. Will Vellacombe and Tom Wills were holding back the horses, who were used to this, knew they should not pull on the hill. No trouble at all. The lantern men at the corner waved them round. They hauled back on the ropes. Gently now. They eased her round the last corner. *Louisa* came round, all her long length, the lamps shining on her. 'Good boys! Steady! That's it! We've done it, we're down!' cried George Pritchard.

It had been much easier than anyone expected.

'Except me,' said Tom. 'I never looked for no trouble, once the ol' boat was well lashed down.'

They halted and took off the safety chains. They took the skid pans from under the wheels. The long hill had worn them bright and sharp as knives, and they were almost too hot to touch.

Still holding her on the drag-ropes they took the life-boat down the last hundred yards of gentle slope. Going easily along, sheltered a little from the wind, with the great hill and the worst of their overland journey behind them (or so they thought) they were in very good heart as they approached the first houses of Porlock town. And here they were brought to an abrupt, unforeseen and dismaying halt.

Here, at the very entrance to Porlock, as if it were going through a city gate, the road suddenly narrowed. On one side of the narrow way was a cottage; on the other a stone wall. There was no way round, and for anything so wide as a life-boat on its carriage, no way through.

The roadside walls up on Exmoor had been quite low, and built of loose dry stones, not very hard to knock down. But this wall here was of rough stones set in cement, and it was six feet high. It bounded a kitchen garden and it was nicely white-washed. It had the hard, solid look of a self-satisfied wall that had stood there forever, and intended to stay there as long again.

The cottage facing it was small, of two storeys, with a thatched roof. It stood out into the road in such a way that it was itself the reason for the road being so narrow at this point. Beyond it, where the neighbouring houses were, the road widened again. The cottage was set at a slight angle, so that the very narrowest part of the passage was just at the uphill entry where the boat-carriage now stood.

The crew and their helpers all came around and gazed at the narrow entry and wondered what to do next.

Tom Wills groaned aloud.

'Old Mrs. Washford's cottage,' he said. 'I'm dead certain she's a-movin' it across the road by inches when no-one's lookin'. I'll take my oath there was more room than this, last time I drove by 'ere.'

They measured the space. The road at its narrowest point between the cottage and the wall was eight feet and nine inches. *Louisa*'s carriage required, for scraping through, nine feet and ten inches.

'So down comes the wall,' said George Pritchard. 'Well, we've knocked down so many this night, who cares about one more. But this 'ere's a tough 'un.'

So they got out the picks and crowbars and sledge-hammers; they moved *Louisa* back a few feet up the road to give themselves room; they set the paraffin flares going to give themselves light; they led the loose horses through to the Porlock side of the road to be ready for putting to the carriage when they got it through; and they set vigorously to work knocking down the wall.

They had been at it hardly more than two minutes when a woman's voice, shrill with indignation, broke out upon the night, louder and more forceful than gales of wind or blows of sledgehammers.

'What d'ye think ye're all doin' at this time o' night? How dare you wake a body up, with all your noise!

What's the time? You leave that wall alone! Who are you? Are you all drunk? Grown men like you, you should be ashamed of yourselves!'

It was the Widow Washford, in her old white night cap, with a grey shawl pulled round her shoulders, poking her head out of her little bedroom window.

To the men working there, after all their night's labours, to be scolded by a little old lady in a nightcap seemed suddenly so funny they could hardly stop themselves laughing.

'It's all right, missus,' Dick Vidler called up to her. 'You go back to bed, me dear. We ain't doin' no 'arm. We're just widenin' the road for the life-boat, that's all.'

'For the *what*?' she asked, in a bewildered voice.

'For the life-boat, missus. Look, there she is, there, up the road. He pointed to *Louisa* a few yards away. The boat looked enormous by the light of the flares. She stood nearly as high as Mrs. Washford's bedroom window. The old lady could hardly believe her eyes.

'Lord a' mercy!' she exclaimed. 'It's Norah's Hark!'

They all burst out laughing at this, and went back to work on the wall, leaving Dick Vidler to explain that although this wasn't Noah's original ark, it was another life-saver of the same kind. She'd never even heard of a life-boat before. Dick Vidler told her that there was a ship in distress in Porlock Bay, and that they were all on their way to rescue the crew.

'I'll get me clothes on,' she said. 'Don't you go till I'm dressed. I'm comin' along, too.'

She had plenty of time to get dressed, for the breaking down of the wall proved more difficult than expected; and when at last it was down a new problem presented itself. On the other side of the wall the garden was not

level with the road. There was a nine-inch drop onto soft soil. It would therefore not be possible to take the wheels out over the line of the wall, as had been hoped. Even if the drop were built up with rubble from the wall there would be great danger of it all sinking down. With the weight of the boat the heavy carriage might cant right over with its wheel down in the soil and its axle-bed resting on the edge of the road. So by knocking down the wall they had gained only the extra room allowed by the thickness of the wall itself, about nine inches. It was better than nothing, but when they brought the carriage up to it they found it was not yet enough. They needed six inches more. Even a little less might do.

Limeburner Purvis patted his hand against the corner of Mrs. Washford's cottage. It was now only this corner, that stood in the way. So Limer Purvis patted the corner and looked at Jack Crockham.

'It'll have to come off,' he said.

'Let Dick speak to 'er,' said Jack. Dick Vidler was generally known to be the best man in the boat for this sort of awkward job.

Dick knocked at the door, and Mrs. Washford, with her bonnet on, opened it at once.

'I'm afeard us'll 'ave to take just a little tiddy bit off the corner of your 'ouse, missus,' he said. 'Now, don't 'ee worry, me dear,' he went on in a hurry. 'It'll all be put back agin, right and tidy in a day or two. Just think of all those poor souls out in the Bay. If us don't get that ol' boat through 'ere, missus, they'll all be drownded.'

'Oh my, oh dear!' she said. Bowman Dick took her and showed her where the corner would have to come off. 'Oh my, oh dear,' she said again, 'there's me little corner cupboard just inside there, with all me Ilfracombe china an' me weddin' teapot. But there, never mind, mister,' she added firmly, 'you go an' do whatever you 'as to. Them poor sailors mustn't drown.'

So two or three of the life-boat crew went into the tiny cottage parlour and helped the old lady move her china and her furniture away from the wall while others began chipping away at the corner with their pickaxes. They had the carriage drawn in very near so that they could tell just how much clearance they needed to make just that and no more. They had the boat-crew ready to rig a tarpaulin around the hole they made, to keep the weather out. But this wall was unexpectedly thick, and no hole appeared.

It was now nearly five o'clock in the morning, and some of the Porlock people, unable to sleep any more after an uneasy night, what with the booming of the wind and the chimney-pots blowing down into the street, were beginning to stir unusually early in their houses. The cottagers just down the road from where *Louisa* was nudging her slow way, inch by inch, along Mrs. Washford's wall, had come out into the road to see what was going on. A hundred yards further on, down at the Ship Inn, the maids were already making up the fires and putting kettles on. Looking out at the windows they saw to their amazement the strange boat, and all the glare of the flares, and all the people and the horses up the road. Wrapping their shawls around them they left fires and kettles to look after themselves, and ran to see the excitement. Farm-hands out of bed earlier than usual to look after their storm-beaten ricks and cattle sheds, turned aside to join the gathering crowd.

There was suddenly an excitement about it all for Derry Larkins. It reminded him of something he couldn't quite remember. The pulling down of the wall, the gathering crowd, the wooden monster, mounted on its wheels, moving in upon the widening passage—what was it that was tugging at his mind?

The big launching wheels were being carefully eased along, one against Mrs. Washford's cottage wall, the other over the rough place on the edge of the road where the garden wall had been pulled away. There it had no

THE SHIP INN
LYNMOUTH
LIFE BOAT

more than three inches to spare. George Pritchard watched it inch by inch, calling out: 'Gently Tom, gently! Easy now!' Derry held his breath. Then as he watched it all, the scene that he remembered came back to him.

'Mr. Stringston!' he said, eagerly, tugging at the schoolmaster's dirty, wet, oily mackintosh sleeve. 'Mr. Stringston, this ain't really like Noah's ark, like the old woman said, is it? D'you know what it's really like? It's like when they took that ol' wooden 'orse into Troy, remember? They 'ad to pull down the walls, because the gates wasn't big enough. It's the ol' wooden 'orse of Troy, Mr. Stringston! And look, they're gettin' it through! It's goin' through *now*!'

And it passed through the walls into the city, and the men harnessed the horses unto it and drew it with them through the streets. And all the citizens stood back in amazement against the walls of their houses as the wooden monster passed by, filling the way.

At the bottom of the road, just beyond the Ship Inn, they took a sharp turn to the left, which was the way to Porlock Weir. Thus they were hardly into Porlock town before they were out of it again, going only through the far end of it. But the news had spread, and there was now a large crowd of followers going along with them. Old Mrs. Washford was well to the fore, in her bonnet and shawl. And people had gone running on ahead to Porlock Weir half an hour before, to tell them there that the life-boat was coming.

The long procession straggled out down the road, going as fast as they could go. They were led by Signalman Morley with his cart. Then came Jack and Dave Crockham and others with their lanterns; then *Louisa* drawn by all her twelve horses; then the rest of the crew and the launching party from Lynmouth; and then tailing along for about a hundred yards the men and women of Porlock, farmhands and fishermen and their wives, coming to help if they could.

Since turning the corner at Porlock they had had the gale full in their faces. It was still blowing hard, and made heavy going. It brought with it the salt spray from the sea a mile away. They could taste it on their lips. In the lulls of the wind they could hear the distant booming of the waves upon the beach.

Derry Larkins had caught up with Billy Pritchard, marching behind the boat.

'Hullo, Derry,' Billy said: Derry noticed that he didn't call him 'young 'un.' 'Hullo, Derry, you'm still with us, then, eh?'

'Yes, o' course, Billy. But I ain't 'alf got blisters. All over me feet.'

'Me, too', said Billy. 'We doesn't do enough walkin', that's what it is. You 'ungry, Derry?'

'Yes, I am. I come out without me supper.'

'Same 'ere. I'd 'ave put a bit o' something in me pocket if I'd known. But in the 'urry I never thought of it.'

None of them had thought of it.

Talking was difficult against the wind, so they mostly kept their breath for walking. But one thing kept coming back to Derry's mind.

'Billy,' he said, the next time the wind eased off enough for him to be heard, 'd'you think the ship's still there?'

Billy didn't answer at first but only shrugged. Then, a minute or two further on, he suddenly turned to Derry and said:

'After all, she's bound to be *somewhere*, ain't she? But then it ain't the ship we come for; it's the men.'

CHAPTER TEN

IT WAS half past five in the morning and they were approaching the sea road at Porlock Weir when they saw a crowd of people with lights in the road ahead of them. They stood across the road and waved them to a halt as they drew near. Jack Crockham went forward to find out what the matter was. He recognized Tom Pollard, the landlord from the Anchor Hotel.

'That you, Jack?' Pollard shouted as they drew near. 'You'll have to stop, Jack. You can't go no further!'

So they halted once more. What new obstacle was this, to stop them in the very last half mile? The roaring sea, now so near at hand, boomed so loudly it made hearing difficult.

'The road's gone!' Tom Pollard was shouting. 'Washed right away in the night! You can't get by to the beach!'

The beach at Porlock Weir was sheltered from the sea by a huge bank of shingle known as the Gore. Centuries of tides and storms had piled it up there. The life-boatmen knew that they could launch the boat there in safety and get her out of the little harbour without mishap. They also knew that it was the only place where they would be able to launch at all. But between the harbour and the place where they now stood the road ran for a short distance beside a stretch of mud-flats open to the sea and covered by it at high tide. Across here the great waves had been beating in all night long, and this was the stretch of road which had been washed away.

'Gone complete,' said Pollard, with finality.

'Well, that's a nice to-do,' said Jack Crockham, voicing very considerably less than the feelings of the others. 'So 'ow did all you people come along 'ere, Tom?'

'Ah, we came along the top lane,' said Pollard, 'but it's very narrow. You couldn't take that great thing along there. It'd never get by, not in a thousand years.'

'Well, I've 'eard all that said before, more than once this night,' said Jack Crockham. 'Tom, it's the only way open to us, so we ain't got much choice. We've got to try it. We'll get 'er by some'ow, Tom, never you worry. So do you lead the way. And you, Dicky, on you go.' This to Dick Morley, who at once set off again ahead with his horse and cart. 'Whip 'em up, Tom!' This to Tom Wills, who called out to his horses for the five-hundredth time that night: 'Come up there, Busko! Gee-up Lady!' And all the team hauled forward, and *Louisa* rolled on again.

'Cheer up, lads,' the Coxswain called out to his crew. 'We'll get her through all right, somehow. Remember Ashton Lane!'

Nobody wanted very much to remember Ashton Lane.

In fact, had it been as narrow as Ashton Lane they would have been at last fixed and done for, unable to do more, for this particular lane sloped up to a hillside with high banks on the left, and dropped down onto a hillside from a wall on the right; and there was no room to turn. But as it happened it was just wide enough for them, within a kissing inch or two of the wheels. They went along slowly and very carefully.

Being now up on a hillside they should have been able to have seen out over the harbour into the Bay. But it was still dark, even if the darkness was now beginning to grey a little, and it was possible to make out, very faintly, the pale white gleam of galloping and breaking waves. But there were no lights or any other sign of a ship at sea.

'When was she last seen?' asked Jack Crockham.

'She showed a flare, must 'ave bin around five hours ago,' said Tom Pollard. 'But since then, there's bin nothing. We reckoned at the time she must have been lying about a mile out, over towards Hurtstone Point. Of course, she may have gone round the Point.'

'She's not gone ashore, then?'

'She may have, Jack, but we ain't heard nothing of it.'

They had now succeeded in bringing *Louisa* all the way along the lane to a point only a hundred yards from the harbour. Here they had to turn off into another short lane which led down a fairly steep slope between high garden walls onto the quay. They were at the brink of their overland journey's end. But at the head of this lane there grew a large and tough old laburnum tree, about twenty feet high. Its trunk leaned out from the wall on one side of the lane. Its knotted branches, all tangled together in thick and twisted shapes, formed a low arch overhead. In early summer this tree made a very pretty sight with its cascades of yellow flowers. But in the early morning of this January day it looked like nothing so much as some black and malevolent old monster guarding the way, waiting for life-boats to entrap. *Louisa* came to a halt in front of it. It was quite impossible to get by, as it stood.

So the immediate answer was, it must stand no more. They must saw the tree down. It was a simple solution, but even this took time and trouble. In order to clear the road to pull down the tree, they had first to unhitch the ten leading horses, take them down the hill onto the quay, leaving the life-boat carriage with only two in the shafts. They were then able to manhandle the carriage back a little way along the lane, thus leaving room for the tree to fall where they could clear it out of the way, bringing back some of the horses from the quay to drag it down the hill. To ensure that it would fall in the best position for this they put a long rope on it, and made all ready to pull it down where they wanted it to lie. Then they set to work with the saw.

While all this was going on Jack Crockham and George Pritchard and some of the others went down to the harbour to choose a suitable launching place. Tom Pollard came running over to them from the hotel close by.

'There's some 'ot breakfast being got ready at the Anchor, boys,' he said. 'You'll surely all 'ave a bite before you launch. You must all be fair starved.'

'Well, thankee, Tom, and it's very kind of 'ee,' they answered, 'but we're very late launching as it is, and I think we'd best not to stop. But a mug of 'ot cocoa would come very welcome to us all, if ye can manage it quickly, for we're all wet through, and it's a cold morning.'

Up at the lane head the laburnum tree toppled down. They got the horses to it and cleared it away. And so *Louisa* at last came down the last few yards of her long night's road, and was brought out onto the quay. They took away the horses and took off the lashings that had held *Louisa* to her carriage ever since Culbone. They hauled her round bow foremost to the beach, and they attached the drag-ropes to the wheels once again. The crew buttoned up their oilskins and put on their life-jackets, and sou'westers, and while they were doing this the people from the Anchor came out with pitchers of hot cocoa. Tom Pollard brought two mugs of it over for Jack and Dave Crockham.

'You ain't put nothin' in it, Tom, 'ave you?' asked Dave, suspiciously.

' 'Eavens, no, Davey,' answered the landlord, 'we all knows about you Crockhams, 'ere along the coast. Drink it down lads, and God bless you.'

So they drank it down, and it was cocoa, and nothing but cocoa, just as he had said. But for all the others there was a good nip of something else in addition.

There were flares on the beach, and lights marking the harbour mouth beyond. George Pritchard and Dick Vidler were already in the boat and had stepped the masts. The others took their places and shipped their oars without further delay. The Coxswain looked quickly around for Ted Pedding, and saw him standing with one foot on the wheel and one hand on the gunwhale, ready to jump up into the boat.

'Go on, then, Ted,' he said, 'in you get.'

The postmaster hoisted himself up and over among the crew. All were set. The launchers hauled the carriage down into the water. Mr. Stringston found himself hauling with them, found himself wading with them into the water, gaiters and all, up to his thighs. They released the keel-chains. George Pritchard took and held the strop. He shouted 'Haul!', and the launchers gave a great haul and *Louisa* shot down the keelway into the water,

and the oarsmen struck all together and pulled for the harbour mouth.

Derry Larkins had gone with a crowd of watchers as far along to the harbour mouth as he could get. He saw for a moment, as they went out under the light, Billy Pritchard pulling his oar in the boat, on his first service. He saw only dimly in the yet unlightened darkness of the morning how the great waves lifted and burst in foam around the boat when she left the harbour and took to the plunging, roaring sea. As she disappeared in the flowing darkness he saw them hoisting sail.

It was half past six in the morning of Friday the thirteenth of January, with the storm still blowing hard. It was ten and a half hours since they had set out from Lynmouth up Countisbury Hill. Who knows how long it was since any of them had last eaten. They had come to their homes all at the end of the working day, ready for their suppers, and to stretch themselves and go to bed. But now it was twenty four hours since they had slept, and here they were just setting out, hungry and wet through from the rain and the sea, at the beginning of another long day's work.

They sailed out on a northerly tack to get well clear of the shore; then they came around with the wind behind them and bore down towards Hurtstone Point; and there, one hour later, as the darkness filtered away into dawn, they saw in the grey spray-mist the grey shape of a three-masted ship lying into the sea, at anchor, with the waves breaking over her. They came in close under her lee and saw a man at her rail; and then Coxswain Jack Crockham hailed through his megaphone, against the wind:

'Ship ahoy! Do you need help?'

CHAPTER ELEVEN

THAT, in a sense, is the end of the story. They had overcome every obstacle; the ship, contrary to any reasonable hope or expectation, was still afloat when they got there; their help was indeed needed; and all their efforts had in the end been worthwhile. What more could one ask?

But in real life things hardly ever finish with fine, dramatic conclusions as they do in books and theatres. In real life there is always something left over that has to be cleared up. Somebody always has to go on and get the next meal. And so (since this is a story from real life) although 'Ship ahoy! Do you need help?' makes a fine dramatic line to bring down the curtain at the end of a chapter, we must here take it up again to finish the story by explaining what happened afterwards. For, in fact, one does ask for a little more.

The ship *Forest Hall* which had dragged her anchors all the way across the Bristol Channel and along the coast of North Devon in the darkness of that stormy night, drifting past Lynmouth, past the Foreland, past Culbone cliffs, getting always a little closer to the shore, past the not very distant lights of the houses at Porlock

Weir, might indeed have finished up under the cliffs at Hurtstone Point, where she would certainly have been pounded to pieces by the sea. As he fired his last distress signal, without hope that any life-boat would be able to launch or get to him on such a night, Captain Uliss gloomily reflected that only a miracle could now save them. Whether by a miracle or not, as they entered the shallower waters of Porlock Bay just beyond the five-fathom line the dragging anchors suddenly took hold of the bottom, and at last did not let go again. The seas at once started to beat upon the ship and plunge over her deck in a terrible fashion; but her iron hull was built to withstand it and she was in a sufficient depth of water (though only just, as it happened) to float without touching the bottom. So there she rode out the night. When morning came the condition of her crew was very wretched. With only fifteen men aboard and many of these now so seasick they could not stand on their feet, she could do nothing at all for herself and depended only on her anchor chains and on the mercy of whatever next might come. And what came next, in the foam of the great, grey waves at dawn, was the life-boat *Louisa* from Lynmouth.

After this it became necessary to get a tug-boat to the ship. As luck would have it, when full daylight came they saw one in the distance. It turned out to be the *J. Joliffe*, the same from which the ship had parted company on the previous afternoon. With the life-boat's help they were at last able to get a tow-line aboard the ship, and some of the life-boat's crew went aboard to help get up the anchors, which the ship's crew were now too weak to do by themselves. So after some difficulty they were able to pull away from the lee shore in Porlock Bay, and they made slowly towards the Welsh coast, with the life-boat in attendance. But it was a hard journey. The ship could not steer herself, and was yawing badly on the tow-line. Besides this, the wind was still blowing strongly, and in spite of anything the tug could do they all found themselves being driven dangerously near to the shallows known as the Nash Sands. The captain signalled for a second tug, and when at last this came the life-boat was still there to help get the second line aboard. And so, with this further help they managed to work their way across the Channel to the port of Barry, in South Wales. By the time they got there it was six in the evening. The whole day had gone by, and it was dark again. And here at Barry, for the first time since they had set out up Countisbury Hill twenty-four hours before, the life-boatmen of Lynmouth ate food and took off their wet clothes and slept.

Meanwhile Derry Larkins and Mr. Stringston and the others who had stayed behind at Porlock Weir, having watched the life-boat as far as they could see her, had gone and eaten a very good breakfast at the Anchor Hotel; and Derry had fallen asleep at the table before he

had even swallowed the last mouthful. They went back to Lynmouth later in the morning, Derry riding in Dick Morley's cart. The life-boat carriage trundled on ahead, without its load. At the top of Hawkcombe Head they stopped and looked back, out over the Bristol Channel. It was a bright day in spite of the wind, and visibility was very clear all the way across to Wales. A long way off they could see the ship, and the smudge of smoke from the tug's long smoke-stack; and once, though it was all too far away to be sure, Derry thought he saw the sunlight gleam on the two small sails of the little life-boat standing by in attendance. Then they continued on their way along the road. They passed a great number of pulled-down walls and overturned gate-posts; otherwise it all looked quite ordinary by day.

The following afternoon the life-boat returned to Lynmouth from Barry. It had been towed part of the way by a steamer going down-channel; after which, with a nice breeze, a choppy sea and patches of winter sunshine, they made their own way home at ease and in good time. A nice day for a sail. When they reached Lynmouth Mr. Oakley was on the quay with quite a crowd to

welcome them. The story of the launch had come back with the carriage team, and was all over the village. The crew were made to feel quite proud of themselves. Then, when *Louisa* had been washed down and made ship-shape, and was back in her boat-house, they all went to their homes just as usual. Take Jack Crockham, for example. He stood a moment in his cottage doorway and saw the tablecloth on the table and the kettle boiling its lid off on the range, and the coloured print of Queen Victoria above the mantelpiece, and *God Is Love* printed in flowers and framed, on the left of the range; and the bellows and toasting fork and kettle-holder hanging up on the right; and he saw his wife putting four spoonfuls of tea into the old brown teapot, and he said: 'Ah, there, me dear, that's just the thing! Just what I'm ready for!' He took off his sea-boots in the porch and stood them carefully aside. Then he went in and sat down at the table, and his wife poured his tea, which he had with a pie of smoked haddock and bacon, and apple dumplings after.

A gentleman in Lynmouth later gave wa tches to all the life-boat crew to commemorate the great occasion; besides which they each received an award of five pounds, which in those days was a goodish sum.

There is something more to be said about Derry Larkins. It may have been thought quite odd that a stable-boy with only a sort of quick lick of an education should in those days have taken such an interest in stories from old Greek literature and mythology. Certainly, as we have seen, Mr. Stringston thought it odd, but a thing to be encouraged; and certainly he was right. But at the time he saw no return for any of the efforts he made. Derry continued to work at Jonas's stables and continued to be happy there, and Ulysses and Poseidon and the walls of Troy were left to look after themselves. Mr. Stringston presently left Lynmouth and went to teach in Norfolk, where in 1915, during the First World War, being now rather too old for military service, he became a head-master at a grammar school.

In the same year Derry, who was by that time a married man with two young children, joined the army along with the other men of his age, and went overseas to France. He was put in charge of horses in the R.A.S.C., where he did very well and became a sergeant. After being wounded at the Somme he was sent on a course to study petrol engines and motor transportation, and from this he became deeply interested in motor-cars. So when he left the army in 1919 with his gratuity in his pocket, he started up on his own in the motor business, with a garage not far from Lynton.

So far so good; and time went by. Some years later—never mind how many—a rather elderly gentleman (in fact, a retired headmaster from Norfolk) was driving his second-hand 1927 Jowett two seater on a leisurely tour of Devonshire, visiting places he had known well when he was a much younger man. One afternoon, as he was going up a steep hill not far from Lynton, he found that his engine, which had lost a lot of power over the last few miles, was hardly able to wheeze its way to the top. But having got there at last the motorist, to his relief, saw a garage not far off, down the road on the other side of the hill. So he rolled along to it and pulled in. The trouble was quickly spotted as a blown gasket.

While the young mechanic was away to see what he could do about fitting a new gasket the garage proprietor came out of his house next door, and seeing the motorist

standing there went over to ask if he was being attended to. Though neither recognized the other at first, each felt there was something faintly familiar. The motorist looked hard at the garage proprietor, then he glanced up at the board over the big doorway and read: LYN VIEW MOTOR WORKS: D. LARKINS, and then he looked back at the garage proprietor who, in spite of being bald, was now after all quite recognizable, and he said:

'Well, I'm blowed!'

'Well I'm blowed!' said Derry Larkins in the same way. 'Well, if it isn't Mr. Stringston! Well, I *am* pleased to see you! Well, come in and have a cup of tea.'

So in they went together, and Mr. Stringston met Mrs. Larkins, and of course there was a lot to talk about, and the afternoon went by very fast. The young mechanic presently came to the door and said the work on the car was finished, and when he had gone Mr. Stringston said:

'That young man, he is your son I suppose?'

'Dear me, no,' replied Derry. 'My boy didn't want to go into the motor business. As a matter of fact, he's a solicitor. Funny how things turn out, isn't it?'

He took down a framed photograph from the mantelpiece and handed it across the table. 'That's him,' he said, 'and that's his sister with him. They're our only two. She's younger, of course; still at University. She takes her finals this year. Classics, that's her subject. Would you believe it? Surprises me every time I think of it.'

'To tell you the truth it doesn't surprise me at all,' Mr. Stringston said. 'I always knew you had it in you. Only when you were a boy you didn't have the opportunity. So it's just waited a bit and come out in your children, that's all.'

'Well, no, that's not *quite* all,' replied Derry. 'It's partly they had more opportunity, yes. But there's something else as well; and that was something *you* did.'

Mr. Stringston was of course surprised, and Derry explained: 'You remember back at home at my old mother's place?' he said. 'You used to talk a lot in those days about how everybody ought to stay at school till they was sixteen, or even longer, not leave at twelve, like in my day. I sometimes used to wish I'd had the chance to stay on a bit longer myself. But there it was, I couldn't, so I didn't bother about it all that much. But when it came to my children, that was different. They were clever kids and did very well at school, and me and the wife were determined to put 'em through as far as they'd go. Of course, they got their scholarships all right, but still it was hard for the wife and me when it came up to school-leavin', and all the other kids around was goin' out to jobs and off their parents' hands. Still it was worth it in the end; we pulled through, and the kids went all the way through to University. I often used to think of you, and how pleased you'd be.'

He stood up and went over to a small bookcase beside the fireplace. From between a motoring manual and a volume on the care of horses he pulled out a little blue-covered book, very much the worse for wear, and handed it to Mr. Stringston. It was *Tales From Homer*.

'Remember that?' he asked. 'I wouldn't part with it for worlds. And come to think of it,' he added, 'you gave me this because of those funny old Greek gods of mine, that I was so daft about. Remember?' He laughed. 'In a way I suppose my kids have got *them* to thank, as well as you.'

Far out in the deep sea beyond Lundy Island, old

Yolus turned himself over and prodded Pozzidon in the back and said:

'Brother Pozzidon, are you awake?'

'I am,' Pozzidon replied, 'but only just. What is it?'

'Only this,' said Yolus. 'I've just thought of something: It's an ill wind that blows nobody any good.'

He gave a contented sigh. Doors and windows along the coast slammed in the sudden breeze, on both sides of the Channel, all the way up to Bristol.

LYNMOUTH, 1899

Such a pretty spot for a hotel, such a nice view of the sea,
And all the new well-to-do houses on the hillside, so nice,
but rather a climb.
So nice in the afternoon to hear the clip-clop
Of the baker's horse in the village street below.
Families waited on daily.
And here comes Nurse with the children,
Back from the beach, safe and sound, just in time for tea.
So nice, such a comfort, after all that.

Such a long journey from London, what with the changing
of trains,
And all the trunks, and the soot, and sitting with our backs
to the engine,
To say nothing of the risk of an accident;
And yet, after all that, now it is tea-time again, and com-
fortable.
Thank God for tea-time and Queen Victoria.
Thank God after all it has all been worth doing.

But every once in a while
When the bad weather keeps the visitors away,

And the hotel people fasten their windows against the
    storm,
From out of the shops and cottages at the bottom of the
    hill
The old heroes come again, summoned once more
By the old obstinate necessity not to take no for an answer.
Ten years they were about it at Troy, and even then,
Even after all that, some got away and went further,
Founded a new city in a distant country.
Made a good job of it, too, though it wasn't built in a day.
It's always the same story, a rough road, more than we
    bargained for;
But after all we've done we might as well do the rest of it.
And it was all worth doing.